HOW TO
EMBROIDER

TECHNIQUES AND PROJECTS
FOR THE COMPLETE BEGINNER

SUSIE JOHNS

This updated edition published 2017 by
Guild of Master Craftsman Publications Ltd
Castle Place, 166 High Street, Lewes,
East Sussex, BN7 1XU, UK

First published 2015 by GMC Publications Ltd

ISBN 978 1 78494 299 1

A catalogue record for this book is available from the British Library.

PUBLISHER Jonathan Bailey
PRODUCTION MANAGER Jim Bulley
SENIOR PROJECT EDITORS Sara Harper and Wendy McAngus
EDITOR Cath Senker
MANAGING ART EDITOR Gilda Pacitti
ILLUSTRATIONS Joshua Brent and Martin Woodward
PHOTOGRAPHER Andrew Perris
DESIGNERS Chloë Alexander and Luana Gobbo

Set in Gibson
Colour origination by GMC Reprographics
Printed and bound in Malaysia

CONTENTS

INTRODUCTION

Embroidery is different from most other types of sewing in one important way. When sewing a garment, soft toy or something for the home – either by hand or machine – it is important to sew neatly, but in most cases the sewing will be hidden. When you embroider, however, you want your stitches to be seen: that's the whole point.

When embarking on embroidery for the first time, you need very little in the way of equipment and materials: just a needle, some fabric and thread, and you're all set. Start by practising a few basic stitches, then build up your repertoire, learning new stitches as you gain confidence. That is what this book is all about: learning embroidery stitches, then practising them, while at the same time making simple items to decorate your home or to give as presents to those you love.

The format of this book is designed to help build your knowledge and confidence. The projects are all easy to make but involve a few simple seams and hems, and this book assumes that you have a basic knowledge of sewing.

The book is divided into nine chapters, with each chapter introducing a new stitch and a project to put that stitch into practice. Each technique is carefully written and laid out in simple illustrated steps, designed to help build your skills. To practise each technique, each project is broken down into clear step-by-step stages, helping to simplify the processes involved. So, for example, after introducing the technique of chain stitch, there is a tea cosy to make, embroidered with a cheerful cockerel motif. Following the last chapter, which introduces you to the principles of cutwork, there is a pretty needle case

to make, providing you with a tangible reminder of your new-found skills each time you use it.

In order to get the most from this book, especially when trying a new technique for the first time, read through the instructions very carefully, then gather together all the materials and tools you will need to complete the project: being organized makes a huge difference. Follow the course from beginning to end, chapter by chapter, or, if you already have some embroidery experience, use some of the chapters as a revision guide and others to build on your existing skills. Hand embroidery is very creative and a lot easier than you might have imagined.

BEFORE
YOU START

BASIC TOOLS AND EQUIPMENT

① NEEDLES

It is essential to have the right needle for the task. You need to choose one that is suitable for the thickness of the fabric and thread.

Ⓐ **Crewel needles** are designed for embroidery, being of medium length with a sharp point and a long eye to accommodate several thicknesses of thread. You can use them for general sewing too – and the longer eye makes them easier to thread. They are available in sizes 1–10: the smaller the number, the finer the needle.

Ⓑ **Chenille needles** are longer and thicker than crewel needles and are useful for embroidery on heavier fabrics and with thicker threads, such as those used for the Baby Blanket on page 48.

Ⓒ **Sharps** are medium-length needles with a small, round eye; they are useful for general sewing. You will need a selection for making up the projects in this book. (Alternatively, you can use a sewing machine, if you have one.) Needle lengths vary: choose a longer one for basting and gathering and a shorter one for stitching seams and hems. Shorter-length sharps are called 'betweens' and are a good choice for fine fabrics and tiny stitching.

Ⓓ **Tapestry needles** have a long eye and a blunt tip; they are available in sizes 13–26. Mostly used for canvaswork and counted thread work on evenweave fabrics (which are not included in this book), they are also useful for threading in and out of stitches, such as the whipped and woven running stitches on pages 24 and 25, where it is important not to split or snag the threads.

② Needle threader

This is a small device that has a wire loop, which is pushed through the eye of the needle to help thread it.

③ SCISSORS

Embroidery scissors Ⓔ, which are small with sharp, pointed blades, are essential for snipping threads and cutting away small areas of fabric. For cutting out fabric pieces, you need a pair of good-quality **dressmaking shears** Ⓕ – which should be reserved only for cutting fabric (never paper) – and a pair of **all-purpose scissors** Ⓖ, for cutting paper and card when making templates. Scissors should be kept sharp. Blunt scissors will make cutting fabric difficult and may result in inaccuracy. **Pinking shears** Ⓗ, with zigzag blades, come in useful for trimming the edges of fabrics that have a tendency to fray.

HOW TO USE A NEEDLE THREADER

Threading a needle can sometimes be frustrating, so it is useful to keep a needle threader in your work box. Insert the wire loop through the eye of the needle. Push the end of the thread through the loop, then withdraw the wire loop from the needle, pulling the thread through the eye as you do so.

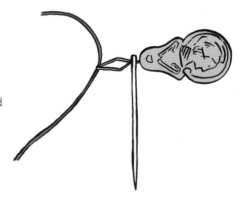

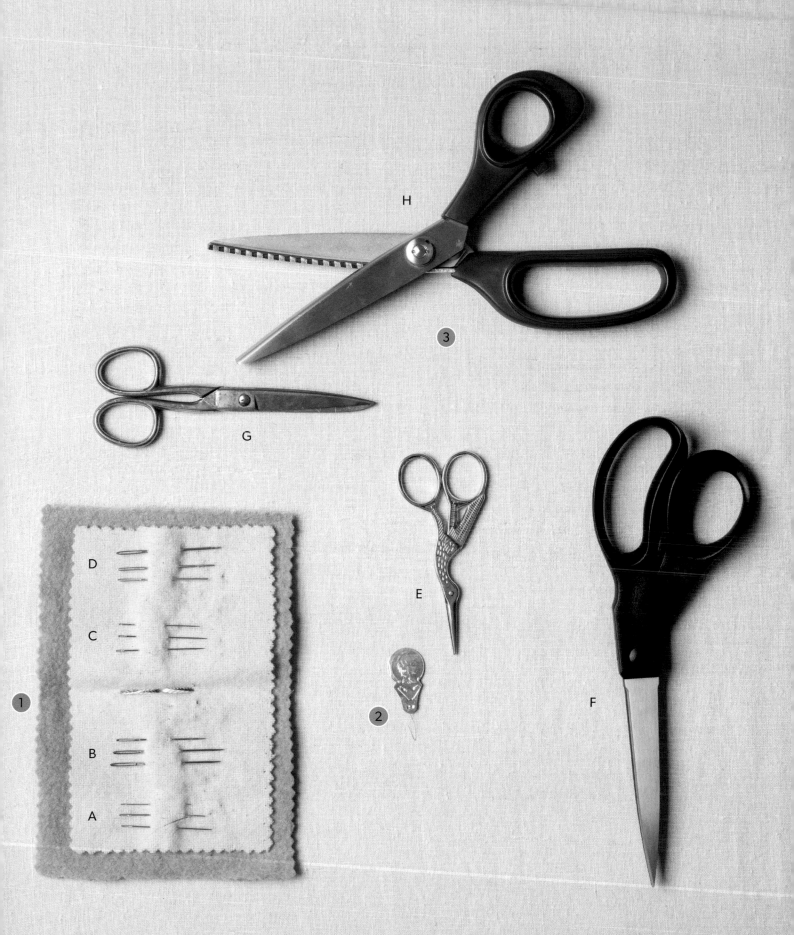

4 STITCH RIPPER

A stitch ripper – or a craft knife with a fine, sharp blade – is useful if you need to unpick a seam or unpick embroidery that's gone wrong. A stitch ripper has a hooked end containing a small blade that will cut threads between seam layers.

5 EMBROIDERY HOOPS

Consisting of two **wooden** or **plastic rings**, the larger of which has a screw that can be tightened or loosened to accommodate fabrics of different weights, embroidery hoops hold the fabric taut. This is important when working stitches that might otherwise cause the fabric to pucker and distort. Plastic hoops that have a **spring clip** instead of a screw are also available.

6 MARKERS

For making marks on the right side of the fabric, which can later be removed, look out for **erasable pens** (I). There are various types with different kinds of ink, some of which simply vanish after a number of hours and others that can be erased with water. For marking the wrong side of most fabrics and for drawing outlines that will be covered by embroidery stitches, an ordinary **graphite pencil** (J) is ideal, or a ball-point **pen** (K).

7 Tailor's chalk and chalk pencils

– with a brush on the end for erasing **chalk marks** – are useful marking tools for drawing pattern pieces and they are available in various colours: light colours for dark fabrics and vice versa.

8 OTHER USEFUL ITEMS

Good-quality steel pins that will not rust or become blunt can be used as a temporary measure for holding layers of fabric together. Keep them in a lidded box. **Glass-headed pins** (L) are more expensive but very useful because they are easier to see and therefore less likely to become lost in the weave of a fabric.

A **tape measure** (M) is handy for measuring large lengths of fabric. You will also need a couple of **rulers** (N): a long one for drawing lines accurately and a small one for measurements such as seam allowances. A **T-square** or **set square** (O) is very useful for measuring neat right-angled corners. A **thimble** (P) is a useful accessory for some sewers while others find it unnecessary or cumbersome. Keep a blunt **knitting needle** (Q) in your sewing workbox, for making neat corners when turning work.

IRONING EQUIPMENT

A steam iron is invaluable for pressing at various stages in the making of a project. When sewing a project, pressing properly is as important as stitching; it helps to smooth out wrinkles, of course, but it also helps to shape fabric and set seams. Make sure your ironing board cover is clean because dirt and scorch marks can be transferred to your fabric and spoil the appearance. When pressing delicate fabrics, always use a pressing cloth. When pressing an embroidered piece, keep a towel handy: fold it to provide a cushioned bed for the embroidery, and press embroidered areas on the reverse to avoid squashing and flattening the stitches.

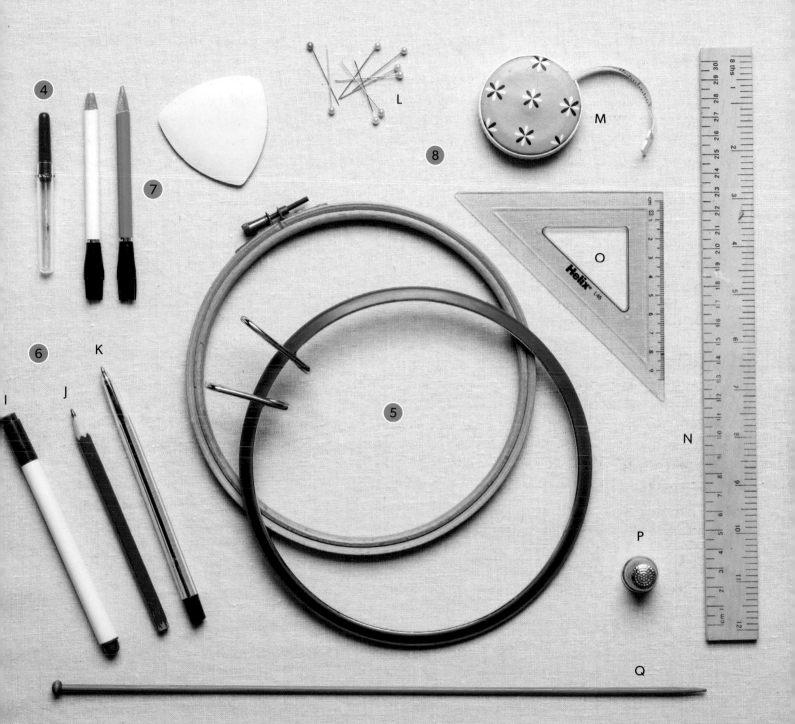

BASIC MATERIALS

FABRICS

The choice of fabrics and threads available for embroidery has grown in recent years, partly owing to internet shopping and partly also to the resurgence of needlework and other handicrafts. Fabrics can be made from natural fibres such as cotton, linen, silk or wool, from plant-based cellulose, or from synthetic fibres.

Many of the projects in this book, such as the Kantha cushion (page 26), the bird picture (page 32) and the embroidered napkins (page 56) use linen fabrics of various weights. Other projects, such as the apron with pockets (page 76) and the needle case (page 94), use medium-weight cotton fabrics. The café curtain (page 86) is made from voile and the baby blanket (page 48) uses brushed cotton.

The reason for choosing natural fabrics is that the needle glides in and out more easily than it does with synthetics. Try out some sample stitches on a piece of pure cotton and then on a polyester-cotton blend. Natural cotton and linen fabrics are available in a multitude of plain colours, stripes, checks and prints.

Before cutting and stitching these fabrics, check whether they are pre-shrunk and, if you're not sure, it is advisable to wash them first. Use washable fabrics for items that will be in regular use, such as a cushion cover or baby blanket – check the information printed on the selvedge of the fabric first to see if it's washable.

1 PLAIN COTTON

This is the most widely used natural fibre. Woven cotton fabric is a good choice for clothing because it is soft and breathable, and feels cool next to the skin. It is a very good choice for embroidery since the needle passes through the fabric easily.

2 PRINTED COTTON

From spots and stripes to florals, zigzags, geometrics, abstracts and novelty motifs, printed cottons are very versatile.

3 WOVEN CHECKS

Evenly spaced stripes along the length and across the width of a fabric produce checked patterns that are practical choices for home accessories.

4 BRUSHED COTTON

A cotton fabric that has been brushed to remove lint and fibres, leaving a soft, smooth finish.

5 6 LINEN

A strong fabric woven from the fibres of the flax plant, usually with a distinctive, sometimes coarse weave, linen is a very popular choice for embroidery. It is available in various weights and thread counts: shown are a fine-weight (5) and a textured medium-weight (6) linen.

7 VOILE

A light, plain-weave fabric made from cotton or synthetics, often used to make sheer curtains.

8 WADDING OR BATTING

A soft, non-woven padding material, available in various thicknesses, made from synthetic fibres such as polyester, or from cotton, and mainly used for upholstery and quilting.

9 FELT

A non-woven fabric made from synthetic fibres such as acrylic, or from wool, which are rolled and pressed together to produce a dense mat.

Tip Before you spend lots of money on items you may not use, ask any friends or family members who are crafters if they have any spare embroidery threads and fabric scraps for you to practise on.

EMBROIDERY THREADS

You may be confused by the varieties of embroidery threads available. The projects in this book use just three different types of thread.

EMBROIDERY THREADS

1 **Six-stranded embroidery thread** is loosely wound in a skein. This thread is very versatile and probably the most popular of all the embroidery threads. Individual threads can be separated and then combined, so you can use any number of threads. The number required will be given in each project. To separate the strands, cut the required length of thread then separate the strands at one end and pull out the number you require, one by one.

2 **Pearl** – or **perle** – **cotton** is a twisted thread with a glossy appearance, which is suitable for many different types of embroidery.

3 **Soft cotton** is a matt thread which is loosely twisted and slightly thicker than pearl thread.

4 **SEWING THREAD**

Whether sewing by hand or machine, it is a good idea to choose a thread with a fibre content that matches the fabric. For sewing up the projects in this book, the best choice is mercerized cotton thread. Try to match the colour of the thread as closely as possible to the fabric; if this is not possible, choose a shade slightly darker. For basting, choose a contrasting colour that shows up well against the fabric, making it easier to remove later.

TANGLES IN THREAD

When sewing by hand – especially with embroidery stitches that involve twisting, looping and knotting – the thread has a tendency to become tangled and knotted. To avoid this, try these tips:

• When threading a needle, use the free end of the thread from the skein or spool and make sure that the end you cut is the end that is secured to the fabric.

• Use a length of thread no longer than about 18in (45cm).

• As you sew, pull the needle in the direction in which you are sewing – usually from right to left.

• If the thread does become twisted, let go of the needle and allow it to dangle, so that the thread spins and untwists itself.

EMBROIDERING WITH AND WITHOUT A HOOP

As a general rule, stretching fabric in an embroidery hoop makes it easier to control the embroidery stitches and achieve an even tension. You can adjust each stitch as it is formed, making sure that it sits neatly on the surface of the fabric. This is particularly important when working satin stitch, because it is formed of fairly long strands that need to be of an even tension. It also helps when making stitches where there are long lengths of thread across the back of the work – such as the scattering of seed stitches and other single stitches on the pockets of the apron on page 76 – where there is a tendency for the thread to be pulled too tightly and the fabric to become puckered.

A hoop is not generally used when working along the edge of the fabric, such as the blanket stitch border on page 48. This is because it is easier to maintain an even tension on an edge, and also because, if you try to stretch a fabric edge across a hoop, it can become stretched out of shape.

For the cushion on page 26, you can choose whether or not to use a hoop, as it is quite easy to maintain an even tension when working running stitch, as long as you remember not to pull the thread too tightly.

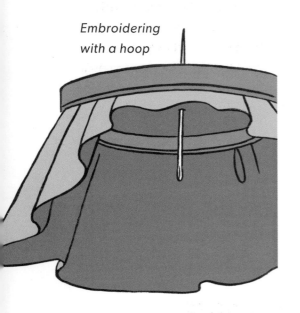

*Embroidering
with a hoop*

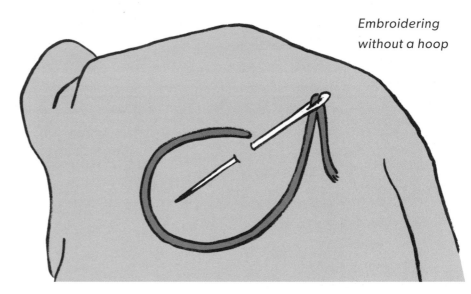

*Embroidering
without a hoop*

UNDERSTANDING THE ILLUSTRATIONS

Use the key below to help you follow the illustrations in this book.

 Right side of fabric A

Wrong side of fabric A

 Right side of other materials
such as interlining or ribbon

BASIC PRINCIPLES

PREPARING FABRIC

Natural fabrics, if not pre-shrunk, should be washed and ironed before you begin your project. This applies even if the finished item is something like a picture, which will not be laundered; washing makes most fabrics softer and easier to work with, allowing the needle to glide through easily.

MARKING DESIGNS

With most hand embroidery, you will need design lines marked on the fabric, as a guide to where to place the stitches. If the stitches will cover these lines completely – as in satin stitch, for example – the lines can be drawn with some kind of permanent marker. If, however, the stitches will be more open, and the design lines will show through, then the lines need to be drawn with a marker that will fade or that can be removed.

For permanent lines, an old-fashioned Biro (as opposed to a gel pen or rollerball) is ideal. However, before using one on a project, try making some marks on a scrap of fabric, then dampen the fabric and rub the marks with your fingertips, to make sure they do not smudge or run.

For making temporary marks on fabric, there are various pens and pencils available (see page 14). The ones that fade away are most useful for small areas of embroidery that are to be finished quickly, since you don't want the marks to fade before you have had a chance to finish the stitching. Lines drawn with water-erasable markers will last longer, and once the embroidery is complete they can be removed with water. For small areas, try rubbing the lines with a damp cotton bud; for larger areas, you may need to immerse the fabric in water in order to remove the marks. Once again, it is wise to try this out on a scrap of fabric first. Some quilters' pencils and tailor's-chalk pencils can also be used; the marks can be either rubbed or washed away.

TRANSFERRING DESIGNS

A lightweight fabric may be thin enough to place on top of a design and trace the lines directly. With fabrics that are less translucent, you will find a light box useful, to make the lines of the design visible through the fabric. If you don't have a light box, however, you can improvise by taping the design to a window: tape the fabric on top and you should be able to see the design and trace it on to the fabric. With each of these tracing methods, you will first need to trace or photocopy the design on to plain paper. An alternative to tracing directly on to the fabric is to make a heat transfer (see box, below).

MAKING A HEAT TRANSFER

You will need a heat transfer pen or pencil and thin white paper (but not tracing paper, which tends to buckle under the heat of the iron). Lay the paper over the design and trace it. Then lay your fabric on an ironing board, lay the tracing face down on the fabric and press with a hot iron. Lift off the paper to reveal the design (which will be reversed) on the fabric.

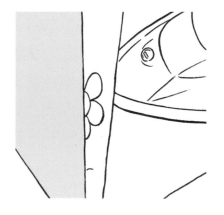

TECHNIQUES & PROJECTS

RUNNING STITCH

THE MOST BASIC EMBROIDERY STITCH, RUNNING STITCH IS ALSO ONE OF THE MOST VERSATILE AND POPULAR, AND THE EASIEST STITCH OF ALL TO WORK. VARIATIONS OF THIS STITCH INCLUDE THE WHIPPED RUNNING STITCH AND THE LACED RUNNING STITCH.

Examples of running stitch can be found in traditional embroidery all over the world. In Bangladesh, for instance, Kantha embroidery is used to stitch together several layers of old sari fabrics, to make cushions and quilts. In Japan, Sashiko embroidery is worked in white cotton on indigo-dyed fabrics.

If you are working this stitch in a hoop (see page 20), use a stabbing motion, taking the needle up through the fabric and pulling the thread taut before pushing it back down through the fabric, completing one stitch at a time. If you are working without a hoop (see page 20), you can work several stitches at a time, taking the needle in and out of the fabric at a shallow angle, with a rocking motion. For joining projects such as the Kantha Cushion on page 26, you can use slipstitch (see box, page 25).

RUNNING STITCH

Working from right to left, bring the needle up to the right side of the work, then back down into the fabric a little way along the stitch line. Bring the needle out again about the same distance along. Repeat this action all along the line.

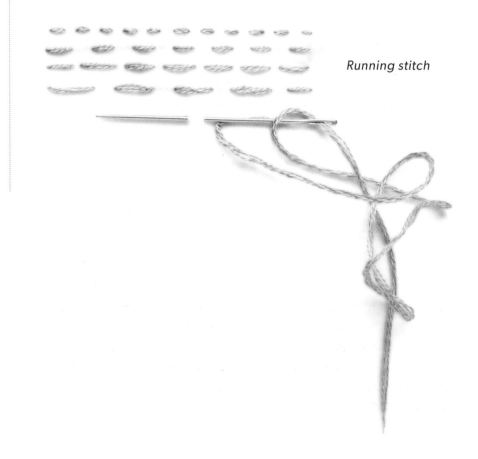

Running stitch

Though the project that accompanies this technique uses only simple running stitch, there are a number of variations to the basic stitch. Two of these are shown here – they are used to decorate the embroidered napkins on page 56.

WHIPPED RUNNING STITCH

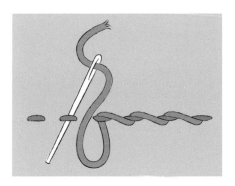

Work a line of running stitch. Using a contrasting colour and a tapestry (blunt-ended) needle, bring the needle up at one end of the line of running stitch and pass the needle under each stitch in turn, always in the same direction, without piercing the fabric. When you reach the end of the line of stitches, pass the needle back through the fabric in the centre of the last stitch.

LACED RUNNING STITCH

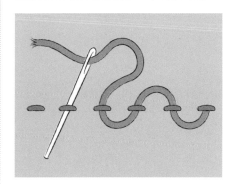

Work a line of running stitch. Bring a tapestry needle threaded with a contrasting coloured thread up at the centre of the first running stitch. Pass the needle under the next stitch from top to bottom, then under the following stitch, also from bottom to top. Repeat, alternating the direction of the needle, to create a wavy line.

SLIPSTITCH

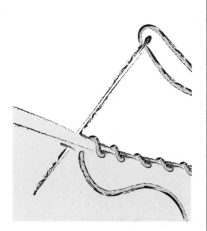

When joining two folded edges, bring the needle out through one edge, then make a small stitch into the fold on the opposite edge. Pull the thread through, then make a small stitch into the fold on the opposite edge. Continue in this way, stitching into each edge in turn and pulling the thread to draw the two folds together.

Tip When working Kantha embroidery, it is not necessary to stretch the fabric in a frame or hoop. You work several stitches at once; the stitch is a running stitch that is slightly longer on the top (right) side of the fabric than it is underneath. You will soon build up a rhythm of stitching and, because you draw the design on the fabric before you begin stitching, it is very easy and quick to follow the lines.

KANTHA CUSHION

MADE USING TRADITIONAL BANGLADESHI TECHNIQUES, THIS CUSHION HAS A CONTEMPORARY
FEEL THAT WOULD SUIT MOST ROOM SCHEMES. IT IS VERY EASY AND SURPRISINGLY QUICK TO
STITCH WHEN YOU CONSIDER THE RICHNESS OF THE FINISHED RESULT.

YOU WILL NEED

- Thin paper for tracing or photocopying (for method, see page 21)
- Plain linen fabric, approximately 18 x 14in (45 x 35cm)
- Erasable marker pen
- Tape measure
- Thermal curtain interlining or lightweight wadding, approximately 18 x 14in (45 x 35cm)
- Pins
- Sewing needle for basting
- Sewing thread in contrast colour, for basting
- Crewel needle
- Six-stranded embroidery thread, 1 skein each in pale pink, pink, turquoise, red, green, grey-green or your choice of colours
- All-purpose scissors
- Coin
- Iron and pressing cloth
- Fabric scissors
- Contrast cotton fabric, for cushion back, 16 x 13½in (40.5 x 34cm)
- Sewing thread to match fabric
- Sharp needle, or sewing machine
- Cushion pad, 14 x 12in (35 x 30cm)

FINISHED SIZE

14 x 12in (35 x 30cm)

TECHNIQUES USED

Running stitch (see page 24)
Slipstitch (see page 25)

Tip Thermal curtain interlining is a good substitute for wadding. Available from suppliers who sell furnishing fabrics, it is a soft non-woven fabric that is used to add bulk to curtains.

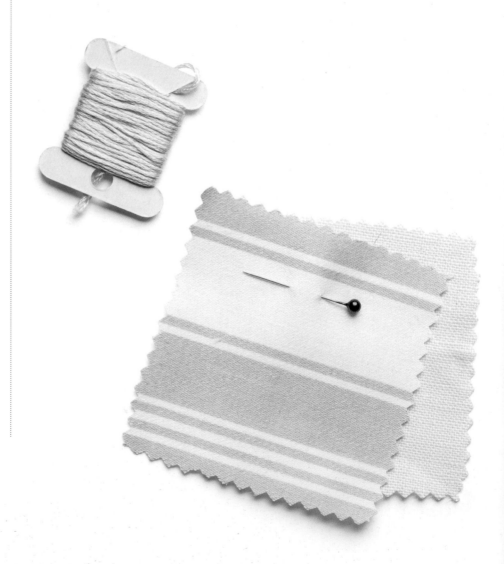

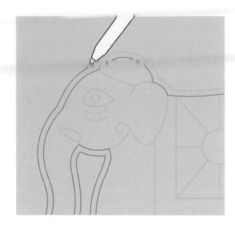 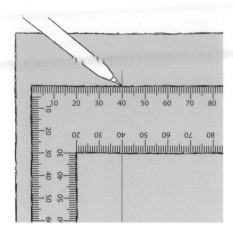 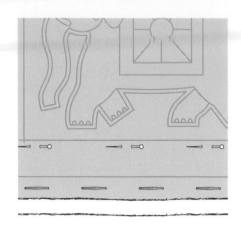

1 Trace or photocopy the design from page 101. Place the linen fabric on top. Trace the design onto the fabric using an erasable marker pen.

2 Using the erasable marker pen, measure and mark a 1½in (4cm) border all round the design.

3 Place the linen fabric on top of the interlining or wadding. Pin, then baste through both thicknesses.

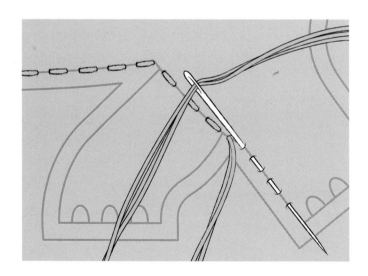 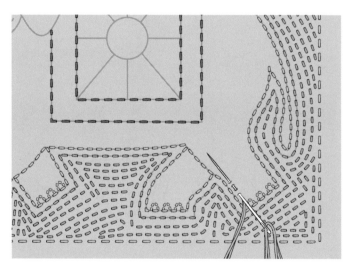

4 Thread a crewel needle with three strands of turquoise embroidery thread and stitch a running stitch all around the outline of the elephant. Thread the needle with green, and stitch lines of running stitch along the inner and outer lines of the border. Make sure that the needle penetrates both the linen and the wadding.

5 Use red thread to outline the *howdah* (the 'saddle') on the elephant's back, then use pale pink thread to fill in the background area, and grey-green to fill in the spaces within the elephant.

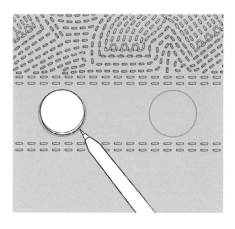

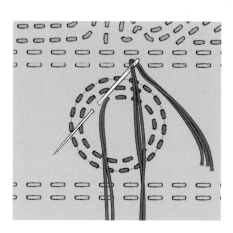

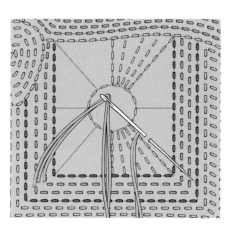

6 To create the border design, place a coin on the fabric and draw around it, then draw freehand wavy lines – or invent your own pattern.

7 Outline the circles at each corner with green thread and fill in the other circles in red, working the running stitch in a spiral.

8 Continue in this way, using the picture of the finished cushion as a guide, or using your own choice of colours, until the whole design has been filled.

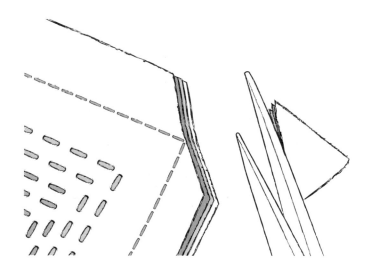

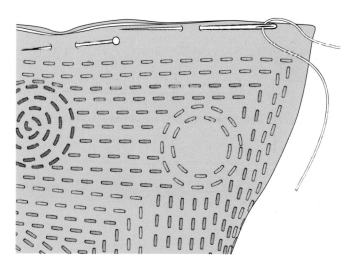

9 Press the work and trim the fabric, leaving a margin of 1in (2.5cm) all round the edge of the border. Place the cushion front and back right sides together and stitch with a ¾in (2cm) seam allowance, leaving a gap in one side for turning. Clip the corners and turn right sides out.

10 Place the cushion pad inside the cover. Fold the raw edge of the material to the inside, then stitch the folded edges together.

OUTLINING STITCHES

EMBROIDERY DOESN'T HAVE TO BE HEAVILY WORKED: SOMETIMES IT'S ENOUGH TO JUST OUTLINE A DESIGN IN THE SIMPLEST WAY. THREE USEFUL OUTLINING STITCHES ARE BACKSTITCH, SPLIT STITCH AND STEM STITCH, WHICH ARE ALL STRAIGHTFORWARD AND EASY TO LEARN.

Backstitch can be used to describe straight lines, wavy lines and curves. It is useful for outlining around the edge of a shape and looks good in combination with most other embroidery stitches.

As well as being a useful outlining stitch, rows of split stitch can also be worked close together as a filling stitch. Stem stitch, as the name implies, is useful for embroidering stems. It is also known as crewel stitch.

In the Bird Picture project on the following pages, in order to vary the thickness of the lines, backstitch is used for the finest lines and split stitch for heavier lines. When embroidering stem stitch, you can alter the length of the stitches and the angle, to create lines of varying thicknesses.

BACKSTITCH

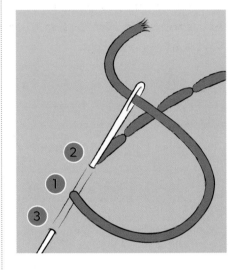

Working from right to left, bring the needle up through the fabric at **1**, a little to the left of the beginning of the line to be worked, then back through at **2**, the beginning of the line. Bring the needle up again at **3**, a stitch length in front of **1**. Repeat the process, going back in again at the starting point, then forward, a stitch length in front.

Backstitch

Split stitch

Stem stitch

Tip In order to achieve even-sized stitches and even tension, and to avoid puckering the fabric, stretch your work in an embroidery hoop.

SPLIT STITCH

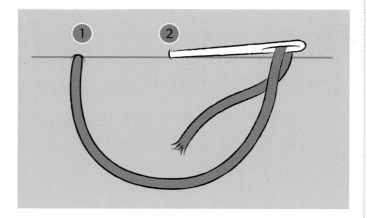

1. Working from left to right, bring the needle up at **1**, the beginning of the line to be worked, then down at **2**, a stitch length to the right.

2. Pull the thread through to form the first stitch, then bring the needle up through the centre of the stitch, 3.

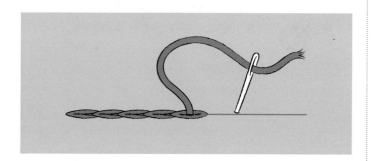

3. Take the needle back through the fabric a stitch length in front. Repeat along the length of the line.

STEM STITCH

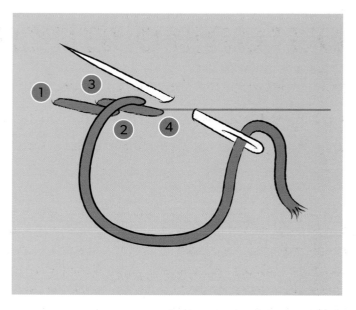

1. Working from left to right, bring the needle up at **1**, at the beginning of the line to be worked, then down a stitch length to the right, at **2**, just below the line. Pull the thread through to form the first stitch, then bring the needle up just above the centre of the first stitch at **3**, and along the line to the right at **4**, another stitch length along.

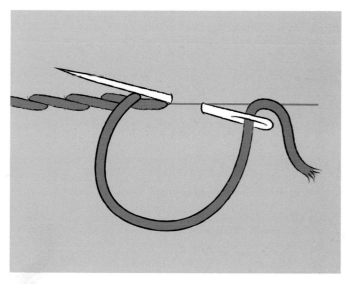

2. Repeat the process along the length of the line. You can vary the length of the stitches and the slant, to make a thinner or thicker line.

BIRD PICTURE

BE PROUD OF YOUR ACHIEVEMENTS: PRACTISE YOUR STITCHES, THEN SHOW THEM OFF. ONE OF THE BEST WAYS TO DISPLAY YOUR NEEDLEWORK IS BY FRAMING IT AND PUTTING IT ON THE WALL, SO TRY THIS PICTURE USING OUTLINING STITCHES: BACKSTITCH, SPLIT STITCH AND STEM STITCH.

YOU WILL NEED

- Thin paper for tracing or photocopying (for transfer method, see page 21)
- Heat transfer pencil or pen
- Fine linen fabric, ivory or white, at least 16 x 14in (40.5 x 35cm)
- Iron
- Embroidery hoop
- Crewel needle
- Six-stranded embroidery thread, 1 skein each in charcoal grey and red
- Fabric scissors
- Lightweight wadding, 12 x 10in (30 x 25cm)
- Thick cardboard, 12 x 10in (30 x 25cm)
- Sewing needle
- Strong sewing thread
- Glue (optional)
- Frame with aperture measuring approximately 12 x 10in (30 x 25cm)

FINISHED SIZE

12 x 10in (30 x 25cm)

TECHNIQUES USED

Backstitch (see page 30)

Split stitch (see page 31)

Stem stitch (see page 31)

1 Place a piece of thin paper over the bird design (see template, page 103) and, using a heat transfer pencil or pen, trace over all the lines. The design will be a mirror image of the finished picture.

2 Place the fabric on an ironing board and place the design face down in the centre of the fabric. Press with a hot iron until the drawn lines have been transferred to the fabric. Check that the lines have transferred by carefully peeling back the paper to reveal the design.

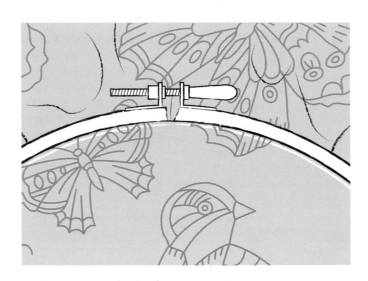

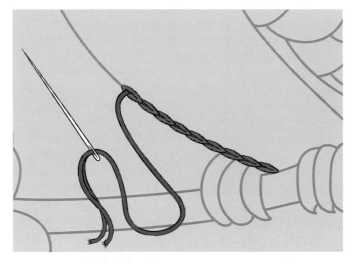

3 Place the fabric in an embroidery hoop. You can use a hoop that is large enough to accommodate the whole design, or a smaller one so you work on one area of the design at a time, then move to another area by repositioning the fabric.

4 Thread a crewel needle with two strands of charcoal grey thread and outline the bird's breast in split stitch.

5 Still using two strands of charcoal grey, outline the stem of the adjacent rose in stem stitch.

6 With grey again, outline the butterfly's wings in split stitch. To create finer detail around the body, head and antennae of the butterfly, thread the needle with just one strand of embroidery thread. Use split stitch for fine lines and backstitch for even finer ones.

7 Continue in this way, altering the number of threads and the stitches to create different thicknesses of line. Use the photograph of the finished picture as a guide.

8 Change to red thread for the rose petals; once again, vary the number of strands and the stitches to produce a variety of line thicknesses.

9 When the embroidery is complete, remove the fabric from the hoop and press on the wrong side.

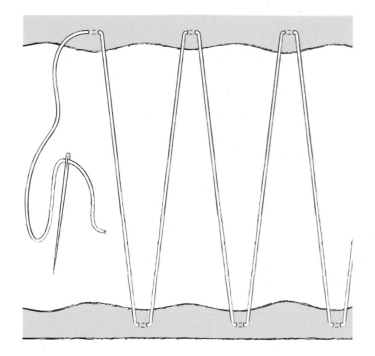

10 To frame the picture, place the embroidery face down. Place the wadding centrally over the embroidered area, then place the cardboard on top. Trim the fabric to give a border of 2–2½in (5–6cm) all round, then fold it over the edges of the card. You can glue the fabric to the card or, to be more traditional, lace the edges of it together with thread. Remove the glass from the picture frame, place the embroidery inside, and replace the backing board.

Tip Using six-stranded embroidery thread allows you to vary the number of strands to produce lines of different thicknesses. Cut a length of thread, then remove the strands one by one. Use a single thread, or combine two or more.

CHAIN STITCH

CLEVERLY LINKED STITCHES INCREASE YOUR REPERTOIRE OF OUTLINING STITCHES. CHAIN STITCH IS EASY TO LEARN, ATTRACTIVE AND VERSATILE. YOU CAN ALSO USE IT AS DETACHED CHAIN STITCH TO WORK INDIVIDUAL STITCHES AND CREATE DETAILS ON YOUR EMBROIDERY.

CHAIN STITCH

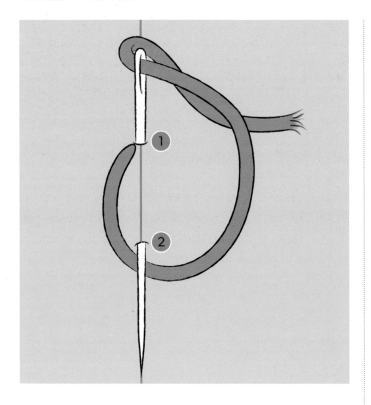
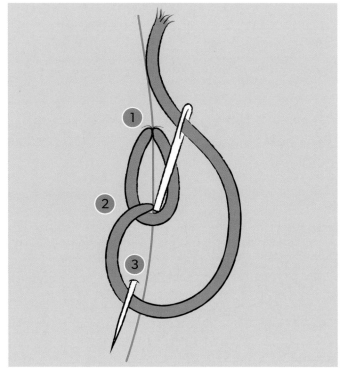

1 Working from top to bottom (as shown), bottom to top, or right to left, whichever seems most comfortable, bring the needle up at **1**, at the beginning of the line to be worked, then back down at the same point and out again at **2**, a stitch length along the line, with the tip of the needle over the loop of thread.

2 Pull the thread through to form the first stitch **1**, then take the needle back down through the loop at **2** and out again at **3**, a stitch length along the line, with the tip of the needle over the loop of thread once again.

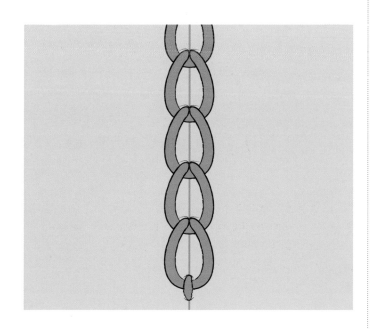

3 Repeat along the length of the line to create a chain of linked loops.

4 To finish off the line, secure the last loop of the chain with a short stitch, taking the needle to the back of the work. Fasten off.

DETACHED CHAIN STITCH

Once you know how to create a line of linked chain stitches, it is easy to work individual stitches, which can be used in a number of different ways, including little flower petals: for this reason, detached chain stitch is also known as 'lazy daisy'.

TEA COSY

CHAIN STITCH IS QUICK AND EASY TO DO, ONCE YOU GET THE HANG OF IT. PRACTISE THE STITCH ON THIS OUTLINE DESIGN OF A COCKEREL AND THEN MAKE IT INTO A PRACTICAL TEA COSY TO ADORN THE BREAKFAST TABLE EACH MORNING OR WHEN GUESTS COME TO TEA.

YOU WILL NEED

- Thin paper for tracing or photocopying (for method, see page 21)
- Pencil or transfer pen
- Woven self-striped linen fabric, at least 16 x 14in (40.5 x 35cm) – see Tip
- Pins
- Iron
- Perle cotton embroidery thread, 2 skeins in variegated shades of orange and red
- Crewel needle
- All-purpose scissors and fabric scissors
- 1yd (90cm) of 1in (25mm) cotton bias binding
- 1yd (90cm) of piping cord
- Sewing thread in contrast colour, for basting
- Sewing machine (optional)
- Sewing thread to match fabric
- Hand-sewing needle
- Cotton fabric, approximately 16 x 14in (40.5 x 35cm), for lining
- Polyester wadding, medium weight, 16 x 14in (40.5 x 35cm)
- Tape measure

FINISHED SIZE
Approximately 14 x 11in (35 x 28cm)

TECHNIQUES USED
Slipstitch (see page 25)
Chain stitch (see page 38)
Backstitch (see page 30)

Tip Choose a textured, medium-weight cotton or linen fabric, in any width, with raised stripes. But make sure the stripes are not so thickly textured that they interfere with your embroidery. Buy 1yd (90cm) of fabric to ensure that you can cut a back and front for your tea cosy with the stripes running horizontally.

1 Trace or photocopy the cockerel design from page 100 on to thin paper. Turn it over and, with a transfer pen or pencil, go over the lines of the design on the reverse.

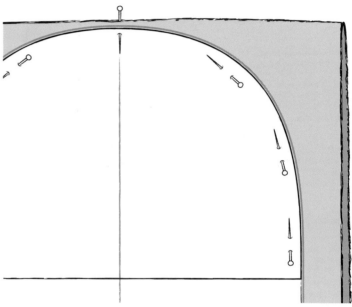

2 Make a template for the tea cosy (see page 100). Fold the fabric in half with the lines running horizontally, pin the template in place and mark out the shape of the tea cosy.

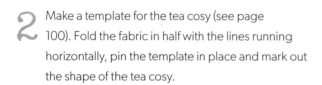

3 Place the paper design, transfer side down, in the centre of this area. Press with a hot iron, taking care not to move the paper, to transfer the design onto the fabric.

4 Thread the needle with a length of embroidery thread. Starting anywhere on the outer edge of the head, begin to work in chain stitch, following the transferred line. Once you have outlined the head, start to outline the body. When the thread runs out, or you have completed one section and need to move to another, take the needle to the back of the work, weave it underneath several stitches and cut off the excess thread close to the fabric. Re-thread the needle and begin again.

5 On the tail section, some of the lines are close together; follow the lines carefully and make the stitches small and even, so that the stitched lines lie nice and flat. When you have completed the embroidery, press the work lightly on the wrong side, then fold in half and cut out the tea cosy shape. Set aside.

Tip You could choose your own motif, instead of the cockerel, to decorate your tea cosy. Just make sure the design is simple, with clear outlines to follow.

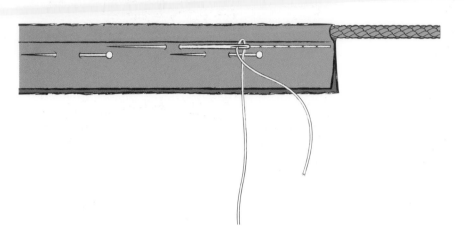

6 Open out the bias binding and press it flat. Place the piping cord in the centre, fold over to enclose the cord, match the long edges and pin through both thicknesses of fabric, close to the cord. Stitch close to the cord, in backstitch, removing the pins as you go.

7 Place the front (embroidered) half of the tea cosy face up on the work surface. Pin and baste the piping to the curved edge, with the edge of the binding lined up with the edge of the fabric, and the cord facing inwards.

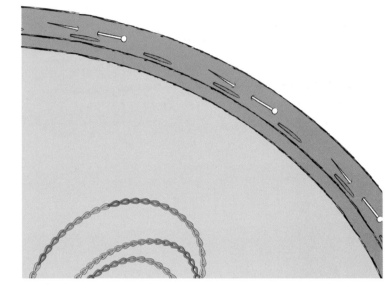

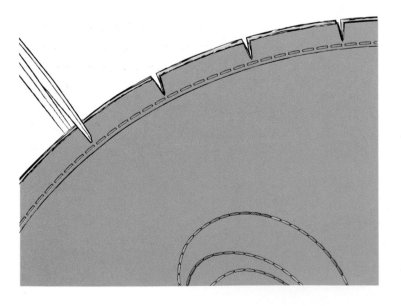

8 Place the two tea cosy pieces right sides together, and stitch all around the curved edge by hand or machine, close to the cord. (If you are using a sewing machine, you need to attach the piping or zipper foot.) Snip into the seam allowance all around the curved section.

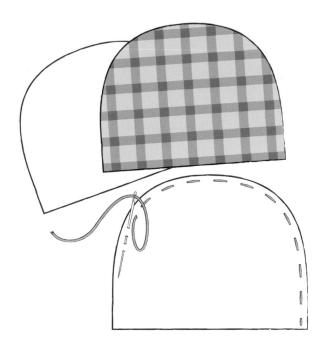

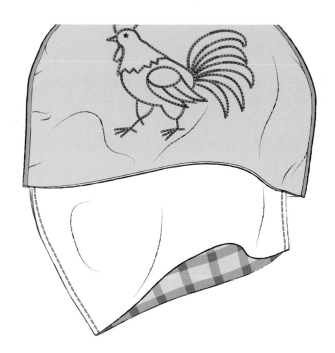

9 Cut two pieces from the lining and two pieces from the wadding, using the tea cosy template. Baste each of the wadding pieces to a lining piece. Place the two pieces right sides together, and stitch all around the curved edge by hand or machine, with a ½in (1.3cm) seam allowance.

10 Cut away excess wadding from the seam allowance and snip into the seam allowance on the curved edge, as before. Slip the lining inside the tea cosy, with wrong sides together.

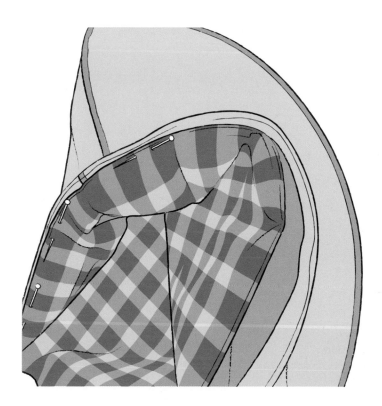

11 Fold 1in (2.5cm) to the inside on the lower edge of both the main fabric and the lining and pin together, adjusting the folded edge of the lining so that it sits about ⅛in (2–3mm) above the folded edge of the main fabric. Slipstitch the folded edges together.

BLANKET STITCH

IN SOME WAYS, BLANKET STITCH IS SIMILAR TO CHAIN STITCH – EACH STITCH INCLUDES A LOOP, WHERE THE NEEDLE PASSES OVER THE WORKING THREAD. IT CAN BE WORKED ON THE SURFACE OF THE FABRIC AS AN OUTLINING STITCH, OR ALONG THE EDGE.

As a surface embroidery stitch, blanket stitch is good as an outlining stitch or as a decorative border. When practising the stitch in the middle of a piece of fabric, as opposed to the edge, it is useful to draw two parallel lines as a guide. When you are confident, you can dispense with these guidelines and also vary the space between stitches and the length of each stitch, if you wish.

Tip When working blanket stitch on the surface of a piece of fabric, it is a good idea to stretch the fabric on a hoop, to keep stitches evenly spaced and to prevent puckering. When working the stitch along the edge, however, you will not need a hoop.

BLANKET STITCH

BLANKET-STITCH EDGING

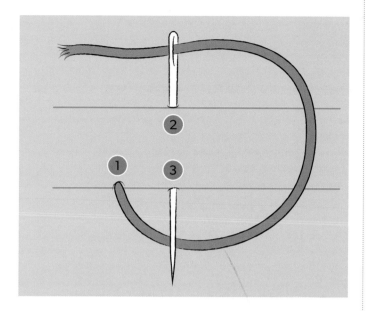

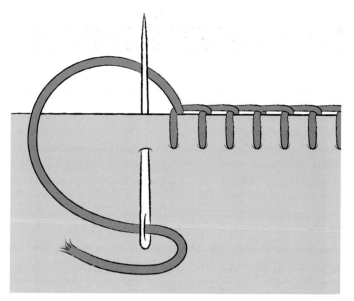

1 Working from left to right (as shown), or from right to left, whichever seems most comfortable, bring the needle up through the fabric on the lower line at **1**, then down into the fabric on the top line, a little to the right at **2**, and out again on the lower line at **3**, directly below, with the tip of the needle over the loop of thread.

When working blanket stitch along the edge of a piece of fabric, whether a raw edge or a hem, the needle passes through the fabric only once on each stitch and the loops are formed along the edge. This example shows the stitch worked from right to left, with the fabric edge uppermost. Try this as an alternative to the direction shown in the other illustrations – you may find it easier.

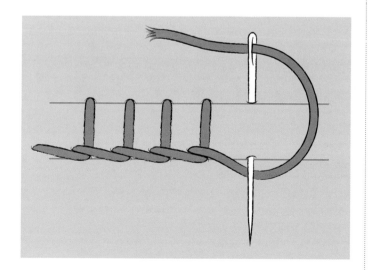

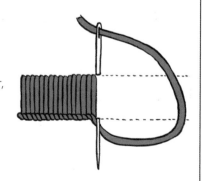

BUTTONHOLE STITCH

When blanket stitch is worked closely, with the upright parallel stitches close together, with no gaps in between, it becomes buttonhole stitch.

2 Pull the thread through to form the first stitch, then repeat step 1. At the end of a line of blanket stitch, take the needle through to the back of the work and fasten off.

BABY BLANKET

BLANKET STITCH MAKES A SIMPLE BUT ATTRACTIVE EDGING FOR A BABY BLANKET. ONCE YOU HAVE PRACTISED BLANKET STITCH, TRY MAKING THIS COSY COVERLET FOR A BABY. ADJUST THE SIZE OF THE FABRIC AND THE COLOUR OF THE EMBROIDERY THREAD TO SUIT YOUR NEEDS.

YOU WILL NEED

- Brushed cotton fabric, plain or striped, 37½ x 30in (95 x 76cm)
- Fabric scissors
- Tape measure
- Crewel needle
- Sewing thread to match fabric
- Iron
- Chenille needle
- 3 skeins Anchor soft cotton, shade 23 (or colour of your choice)

FINISHED SIZE

37½ x 30in (95 x 76cm) or your choice of size

TECHNIQUES USED

Blanket stitch (see page 47)
Running stitch (see page 24)

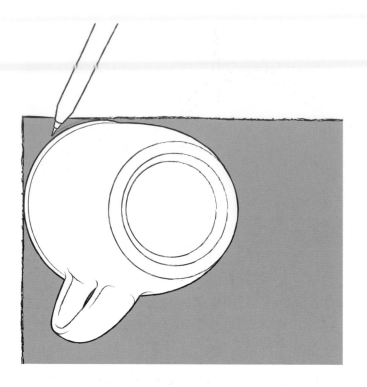

1 Cut the fabric to size, then round off each corner. To do this, draw around a circular object, such as a cup or saucer. Fold a ½in (1.3cm) single hem to the wrong side and press.

2 Thread a crewel needle with sewing thread and stitch the hem in place with a neat running stitch, about ⅛in (2–3mm) from the raw edge. Press again.

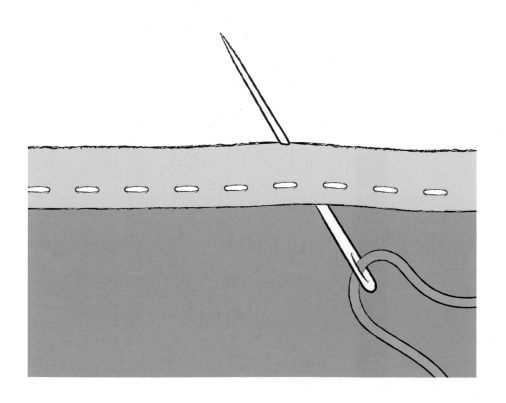

3 Thread a chenille needle with embroidery thread and knot the end. Take the needle up through the hem so that the knot rests under the fold of fabric.

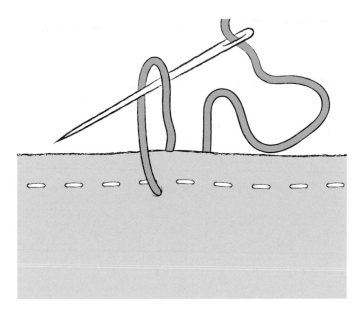 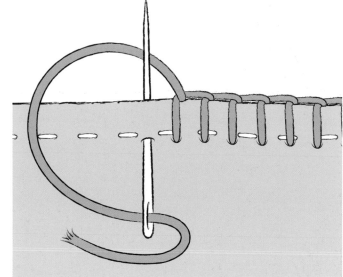

4 With right side facing, take the needle back into the fabric slightly to the left and ½in (1.3cm) down – in line with the lower fold of the hem – and up through the loop of thread. Pull up to form the first stitch.

5 Continue like this, working blanket stitch all along the edge. Keep the stitches evenly spaced – about ½in (1.3cm) apart – and perpendicular to the edge.

6 When you come to a corner, keep the stitches evenly spaced and perpendicular, as before.

Tip When a length of thread runs out, take the needle back into the fold of the hem and fasten off the thread, then start a new length of thread, as described in step 3.

SURFACE STITCHES

STITCHES THAT CAN BE WORKED IN ANY DIRECTION AND ON ALMOST ANY KIND OF FABRIC ARE GROUPED UNDER THE HEADING OF 'SURFACE' STITCHES. ONCE YOU ARE CONFIDENT WITH THE STITCHES IN THE PREVIOUS SECTIONS, YOU ARE READY TO EXPAND YOUR REPERTOIRE.

Herringbone stitch is a criss-cross stitch that works particularly well as a decorative border. When practising the stitch, it is useful to draw two parallel lines as a guide. When you are confident, you can dispense with these guidelines and vary the space between stitches and the length of each stitch, if you wish.

You can also add small stitches across the point where the threads cross: this is called tied herringbone stitch and not only does it look decorative – especially when the tied stitches are made in a contrasting colour – but it also helps to hold down the stitches and prevent snagging.

Feather stitch is a loopy stitch that can be used for outlines and borders, and even for filling shapes. It is usually worked in a vertical line, from top to bottom. When you are learning the stitch, it is useful to draw a set of three evenly spaced lines to follow. You can work the stitches in a row or offset them for a wider border pattern; this is offset feather stitch. To produce a broader line of stitches that are slightly offset from the centre line, draw four guidelines instead of three. In this version, the stitches form more of a zigzag shape.

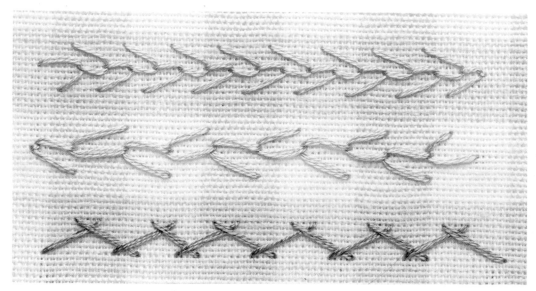

Feather stitch

Offset feather stitch

Herringbone stitch

HERRINGBONE STITCH

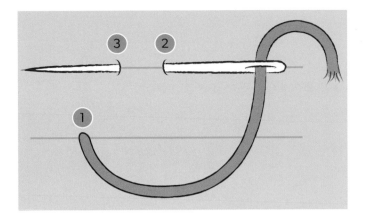 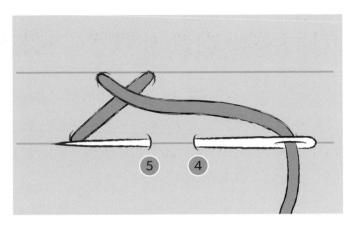

1 Working from left to right, bring the needle up through the fabric on the lower line at **1**, then down into the fabric on the top line at **2**, a little to the right and out again on the top line at **3**, slightly to the left.

2 Pull the thread through, then insert the needle on the lower line, a little to the right and take a small stitch to the left, on the lower line, from **4** to **5**.

3 Repeat this process as required.

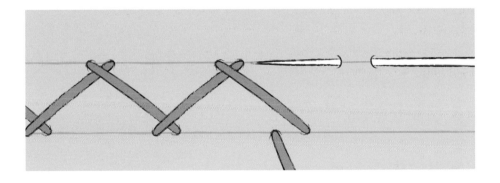

TIED HERRINGBONE STITCH

1 After completing a row of herringbone stitches, thread the needle with a contrasting colour. Bring the needle through to the right side just above the point where the threads cross and make a small vertical stitch. Repeat this along the row, top and bottom.

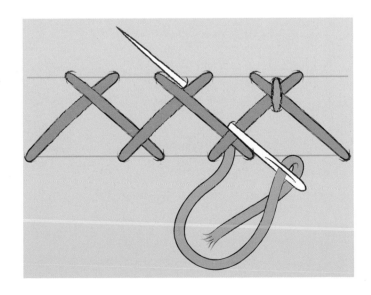

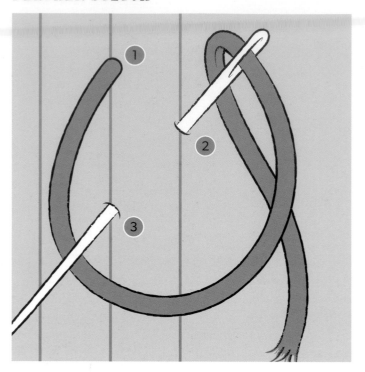

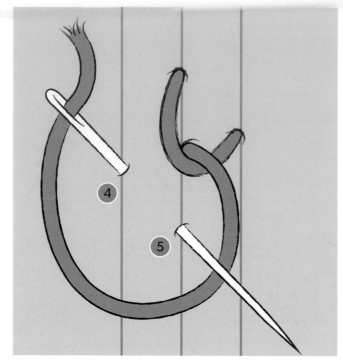

1   Bring the needle out at **1**, at the top of the middle line, then insert it to the right at **2**, a little way down. Bring it up again on the centre line at **3**, a little way down, making sure the loop of thread goes under the tip of the needle. Pull through.

2   Take the needle across to the left and insert it on the left-hand line at **4**, then bring it back out on the centre line at **5**, a little way down, making sure the loop of thread is under the needle tip. Pull through.

3   Repeat steps 1 and 2, making looped stitches on alternate sides of the centre line and making sure each time that you catch the loop of thread under the needle.

Tip These stitches are worked from top to bottom but you can turn the page to view the step-by-step pictures from a different angle, then try working from bottom to top or from right to left to see what suits you best.

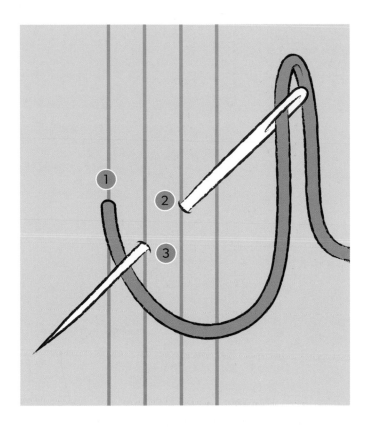

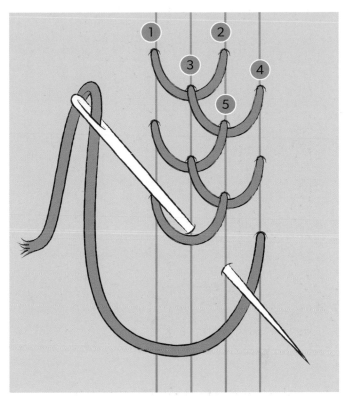

OFFSET FEATHER STITCH

1 Bring the needle out at the far left at **1**, then across to the third line at **2** and back out on the second line at **3**, slightly further down, with the loop of thread under the tip of the needle.

2 Pull the thread through, to form the first stitch, then take the needle across to the fourth line at **4** and out again on the third line at **5**, with the loop of thread under the tip of the needle. Continue like this, alternating between the two central lines to offset the stitches.

Tip In the illustrations on this page, the stitches are evenly spaced but you can create different effects by varying the distance between the guidelines and by working the stitches closer together or further apart.

EMBROIDERED NAPKINS

TRY OUT SURFACE STITCHES IN NEAT ROWS ON SQUARES OF LINEN FABRIC. THIS IS A GREAT WAY TO PRACTISE YOUR EMBROIDERY SKILLS, AND AS A BONUS, THEY MAKE ATTRACTIVE TABLE NAPKINS. FOLLOW THE PATTERNS SHOWN HERE OR MIX AND MATCH YOUR FAVOURITE STITCHES.

YOU WILL NEED
- Linen fabric squares of 17½in (44.5cm) – see instructions for cutting out
- Fabric scissors
- Crewel needle
- Six-stranded embroidery thread in several colours, to tone with fabric
- Tape measure

FINISHED SIZE
Each napkin measures 17½in (44.5cm), including fringed edges

TECHNIQUES USED
Running stitch (see page 24)
Whipped running stitch (see page 25)
Laced running stitch (see page 25)
Herringbone stitch (see page 52)
Tied herringbone stitch (see page 53)
Feather stitch (see page 54)

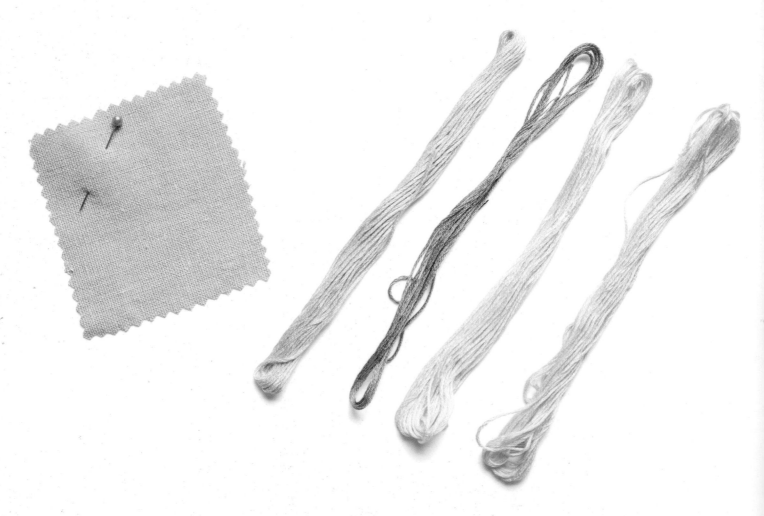

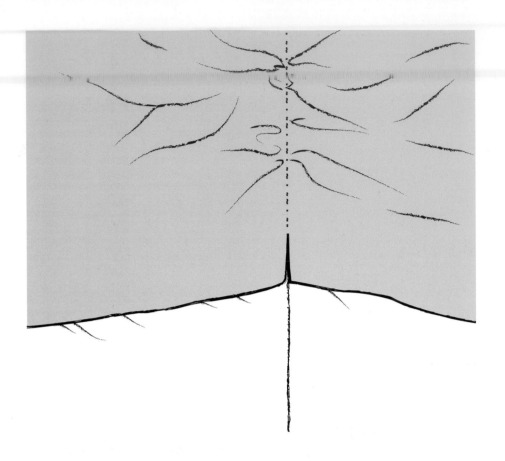

1 Trim off any selvedges (see Tip) from the fabric. Measure out the squares. To make sure the edges are completely straight, follow the weave of the fabric. To do this, snip into the edge of the fabric at the beginning of each cutting line and pull out a single thread.

2 Where you have removed the thread, you will see a faint line – a small gap between the threads on either side. Cut carefully along this line.

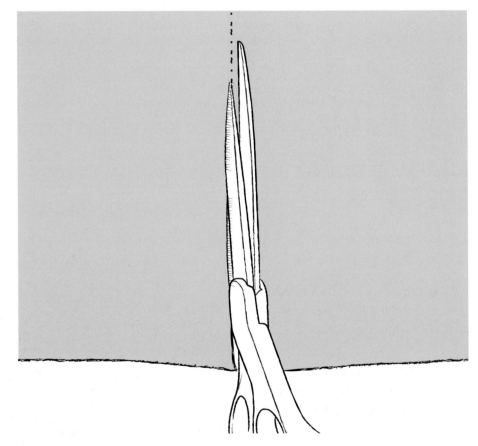

Tip A selvedge is the woven edge of a fabric that prevents it unravelling. You will need to trim away any selvedges before measuring and cutting the napkins because a selvedge cannot be frayed.

3   Thread a crewel needle with three strands of thread and bring the needle up at one corner, approximately 1in (2.5cm) from the edge. Leave a short tail of thread at the back of the work, then embroider a running stitch parallel to the cut edge, making your stitches as even as possible. Make sure your embroidered line follows the line of one of the threads in the fabric.

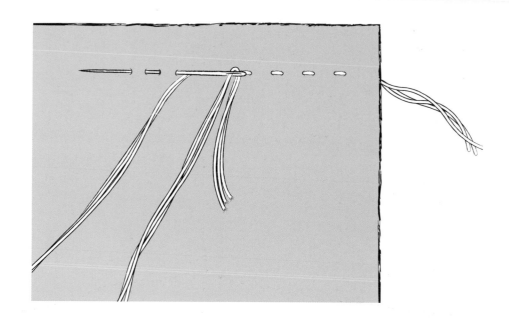

4   Embroider a second line of running stitch about ½in (1.3cm) from the first, all around the square.

5   Whenever you need to rethread the needle, leave a short tail of thread on the back of the work, then knot the new tail securely to the old tail and trim off the ends. When you have sewn all the way round the napkin, tie the final tail to the first one.

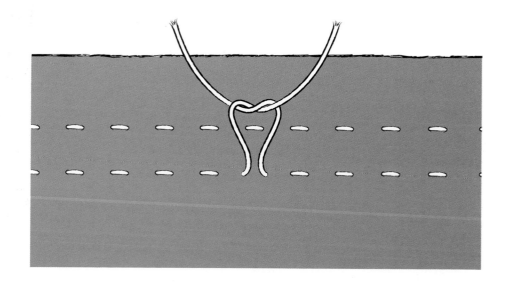

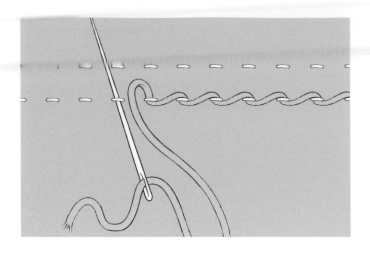

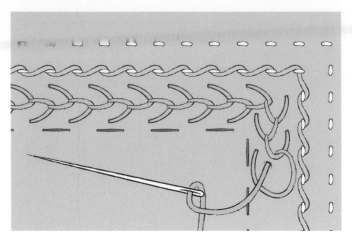

6   For an interesting variation, you can 'whip' the running stitches, using three strands of thread in a contrasting colour.

7   Next, stitch a border of feather stitch parallel to the whipped running stitch. To sew a straight line, follow the weave of the fabric. You could also stitch a line of running stitches as a guideline, using a sewing thread that shows up well on the fabric and can be removed once the embroidery is complete.

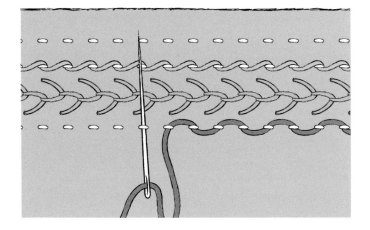

8   Now rethread your needle with a different colour and embroider another row of running stitch. Instead of whipping the stitches, you can 'lace' them. This means changing the direction each time you take the needle under a stitch, to create a wavy line.

WORKING THE EMBROIDERY

The embroidery on these napkins is worked without the use of a hoop. This is because it is impractical to stretch a cut edge of fabric in a hoop. You will need to take extra care to keep stitches even and avoid pulling the thread too tightly as this may pucker the fabric. If you prefer to work the embroidery using a hoop, do not cut out the napkins but mark out their outlines on your fabric. Stretch the area to be stitched in the hoop and when you have completed all the embroidered borders, you can then cut out the napkins and fray the edges.

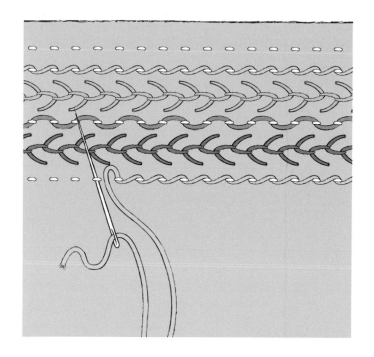

9 Embroider another row of feather stitch in a contrasting colour, then another row of whipped running stitch, to complete the border. On some napkins, you could vary the border stitch, using herringbone or tied herringbone stitch.

10 Pull out threads from each edge of the fabric, up to the first line of running stitches, to create a fringed effect all round the napkins.

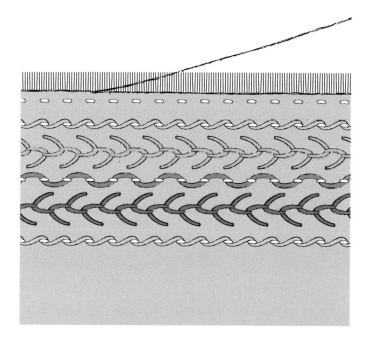

Tip When working whipped or laced stitches, use a blunt-tipped (tapestry) needle, as this makes it easier to work under stitches without splitting the threads.

FILLING STITCHES

ONE OF THE RICHEST SURFACE EMBROIDERY STITCHES IS SATIN STITCH, USED TO FILL AREAS SO THAT THE FABRIC BENEATH DOES NOT SHOW THROUGH. SPLIT STITCH AND CHAIN STITCH (SEE PAGES 31 AND 38) CAN ALSO BE WORKED IN CLOSE ROWS AS FILLING STITCHES.

It is advisable to use a hoop when working satin stitch and its variations, to create a neat, even result and to prevent the fabric from puckering. First, draw an outline of the shape to be filled. When you are stitching, take the needle in and out of the fabric just outside the outline, so that it ends up covered by the stitches.

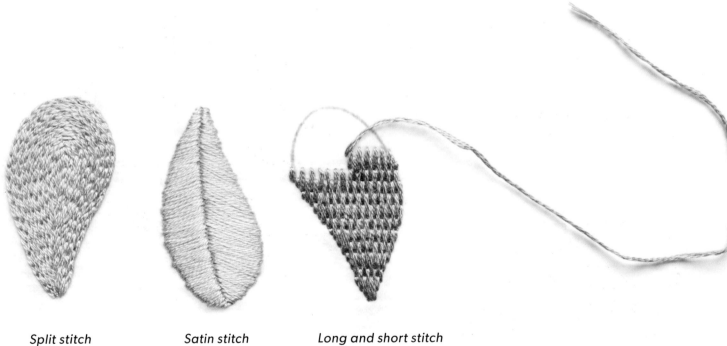

Split stitch   *Satin stitch*   *Long and short stitch*

SATIN STITCH

Satin stitches should be close together and parallel, with no gaps between them, to create a solid area of colour. They should also be kept quite short so they do not snag or pull, so make sure that shapes to be filled are quite small.

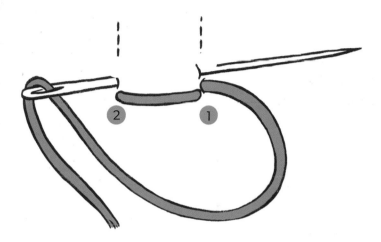

1 Working from right to left, or from bottom to top as shown here, bring the needle up through the fabric on the right side of the shape at **1**, just outside the drawn line, then down into the fabric at **2**. Pull the thread through, then bring the needle back out right next to the first stitch at **1**. Bring the needle down right next to the first stitch at **2**.

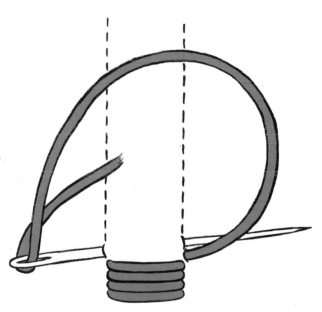

2 Repeat this process, keeping the stitches close together and covering the drawn outline.

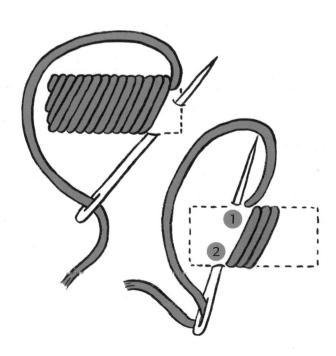

3 Satin stitch can be worked at a slant. For some shapes, instead of starting at one end of the shape, you may find it easier to start in the centre and work outwards, in two stages. This can help to keep the stitches parallel.

PADDED SATIN STITCH

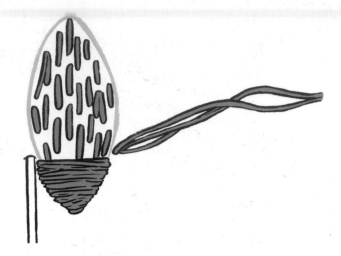

For a richer, more raised effect, first pad out the shape to be filled with small stitches such as running stitch. Work these stitches in lines in a different direction from the satin stitch. So for a leaf shape, for example, you might work the padding stitches along the length of the shape and the satin stitches across the shape.

EVEN STITCHES

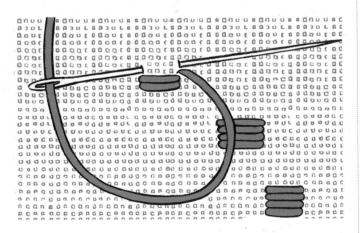

If you are working on an evenweave fabric, you can follow the weave of the fabric to help keep the stitches evenly spaced and of a uniform length.

LONG AND SHORT STITCH

For larger shapes, use long and short stitch, a variation of satin stitch. It can be worked in several colours or different shades of the same colour.

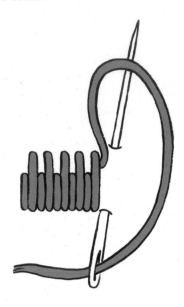

1 Work the first row in alternating long and short stitches.

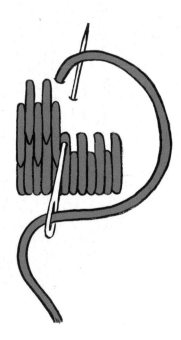

2 Work the second and subsequent rows in stitches that are all the same length as each other, taking the needle into the end of the stitch above, so that alternate stitches will be offset, or 'stepped'.

TATTOO-MOTIF SHIRT

IN THIS PROJECT, YOU'LL EMBELLISH A PLAIN SHIRT WITH A RICHLY EMBROIDERED MOTIF
INSPIRED BY TRADITIONAL TATTOO DESIGNS. THE MOTIF IS WORKED USING A COMBINATION
OF SPLIT STITCH TO FILL IN THE LARGER AREAS AND SATIN STITCH FOR SMALLER AREAS.

YOU WILL NEED

- Thin paper for tracing or photocopying
  (for transfer method, see page 21)
- Heat transfer pencil or pen
- Iron
- Plain cotton or linen shirt, washed
  and ironed
- Embroidery hoop
- Crewel needle
- Six-stranded embroidery thread:
  1 skein each in blue, yellow, red,
  green, white and black
- All-purpose scissors

TECHNIQUES USED

Split stitch (see page 31)

Satin stitch (see page 63)

Padded satin stitch (see page 64)

Long and short stitch (see page 64)

Tip If you are using a new shirt,
it is a good idea to wash and iron it
before embroidering. This will allow
for any shrinkage and will also help
to soften the fabric so that the needle
passes through more easily.

1 Trace or photocopy the tattoo motif from page 98 on to a sheet of thin paper. On the back of the paper, trace over the lines of the design using a transfer pencil or pen. Place the paper, transfer side down, on the front of the shirt where you want the motif to appear. Press with a hot iron, taking care not to move the paper, to transfer the design on to the fabric of the shirt.

2 Place the fabric in an embroidery hoop so that the whole design fits into the hoop. Thread a crewel needle with three strands of blue embroidery thread. Bring the needle up through the fabric at the edge of the wing, in the centre of the design, and work an outline of split stitch along one edge of the shape.

3 Work further rows of split stitch, close to each other, to fill in the shape.

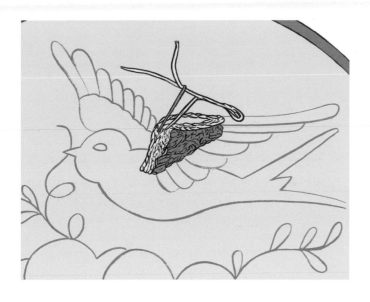

4 Thread the needle with three strands of yellow and use it to outline the other part of the wing, then to fill the shape with close rows of split stitch.

5 Thread the needle with three strands of white and use it to fill in each feather with padded satin stitch.

6 Thread the needle with three strands of blue and outline the body of the bird in split stitch, then work further rows of split stitch, close to each other, to fill in the shape.

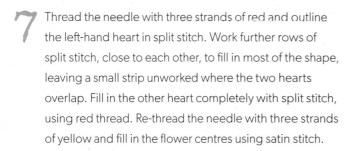

7 Thread the needle with three strands of red and outline the left-hand heart in split stitch. Work further rows of split stitch, close to each other, to fill in most of the shape, leaving a small strip unworked where the two hearts overlap. Fill in the other heart completely with split stitch, using red thread. Re-thread the needle with three strands of yellow and fill in the flower centres using satin stitch.

8 Re-thread the needle with red and fill in the flower petals in satin stitch, working from the tip of the petal towards the flower centre. Thread the needle with white and outline the flower petals in split stitch.

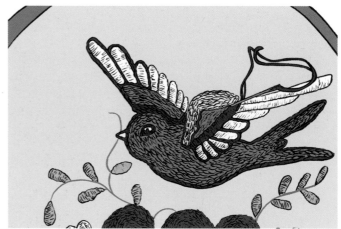

9 Thread the needle with green and fill in each leaf shape in padded satin stitch.

10 Thread the needle with two strands of black thread and outline all the main shapes in split stitch. Add areas of shading in long and short stitch, using the picture of the finished embroidery as a guide. Remove the work from the hoop and press the embroidered area lightly on the reverse, using a steam iron.

SINGLE STITCHES

SINGLE OR 'DETACHED' STITCHES ARE USEFUL FOR COVERING AN AREA WITH PATTERN AND TEXTURE. THERE ARE SEVERAL COMMONLY USED FOR THIS PURPOSE: YOU HAVE ALREADY ENCOUNTERED DETACHED CHAIN STITCH (PAGE 39) AND HERE ARE A FEW MORE TO LEARN.

It is important to choose the right fabric: scattered stitches are best worked on an opaque fabric because the thread is carried across the back of the work, from one stitch to another. If the fabric is too fine or transparent, the threads on the back will show through from the front and spoil the appearance of the finished piece of embroidery.

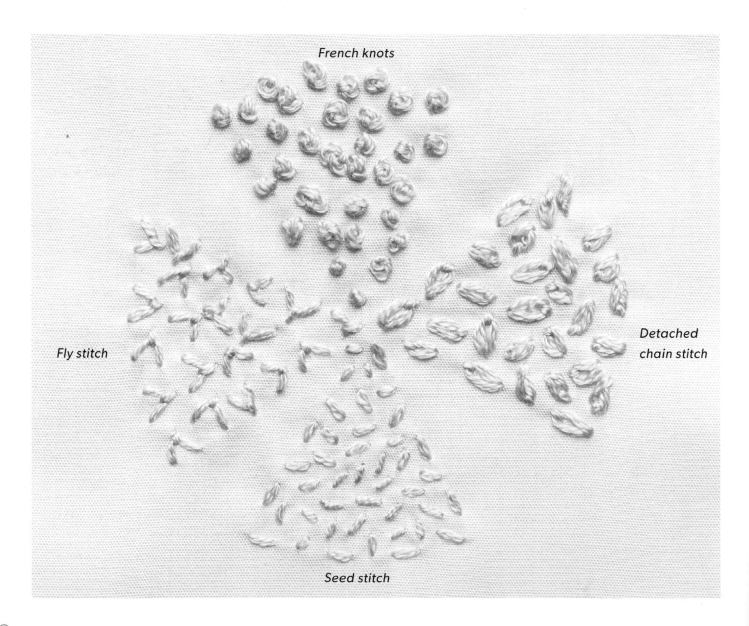

French knots

Fly stitch

Detached chain stitch

Seed stitch

STRAIGHT STITCH

Straight stitch is simply a single straight stitch.

1 Bring the thread up through the fabric and down again in the direction you wish the stitch to lie. You can work the stitches in a row, like this, to suggest grass.

2 You can also work straight stitches radiating out from a central circle, to create small flowers.

SEED STITCH

Short straight stitches are known as seed stitches because they resemble small seeds.

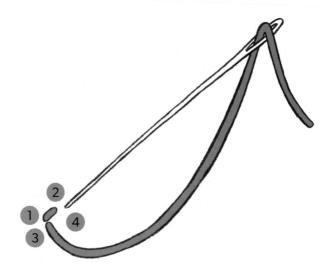

1 Bring the thread up through the fabric at **1** and down again a short distance away at **2**, in the direction you wish the stitch to lie. You can work a single stitch or, to create a double seed stitch, make a second stitch parallel to the first, right next to it and of the same length, from **3** to **4**.

2 When using seed stitches for filling an area, space them evenly and work them in different directions.

FLY STITCH

Fly stitch is a little looped stitch that can be used to suggest flying birds. You can easily vary the size of the stitch and the length of the straight stitch that holds down the loop.

Bring the thread up through the fabric at **1** and hold it down with your thumb or finger; take the needle back through the fabric a small distance away at **2**, then back up between the two points and a little way down at **3**. Make sure that the loop of thread is under the tip of the needle and pull the thread through, then take the needle back into the fabric a little way below at **4**, to complete the stitch. Take the needle up through the fabric where you want the next stitch to be.

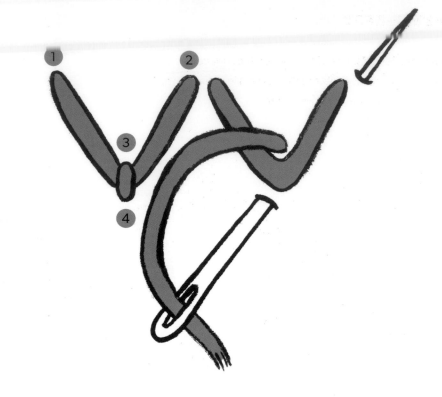

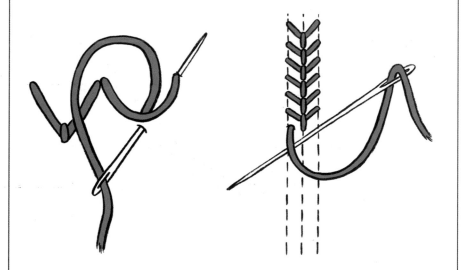

FLY STITCH VARIATIONS

As well as working individual fly stitches scattered in a random pattern, you can also work them next to one another in a horizontal row.

To work fly stitch in a vertical row, draw three parallel guidelines, or use the weave of the fabric as a guide to help keep the row straight.

Tip Stretch your fabric in a hoop before starting to embroider. Because the thread is carried across the back of the work, from one stitch to the next, if you don't use a hoop and you pull the thread too tightly, the fabric will become puckered and distorted. Using a hoop helps to maintain an even tension.

FRENCH KNOT

French knot stitch forms a little knot on the surface of the fabric. These are invaluable for fine details in embroidery, such as eyes on faces or flower centres.

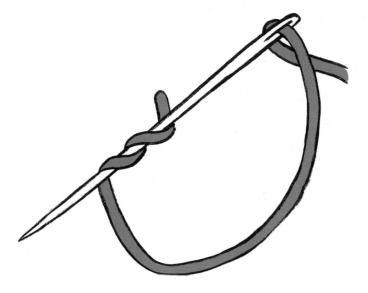

1 Bring the needle up through the fabric at the position of the knot. Hold the thread taut between your finger and thumb, take the needle under the thread and wrap it around two or three times.

2 Still holding the thread taut, take the needle back through the starting place and pull through to the back, leaving a small knot on the surface.

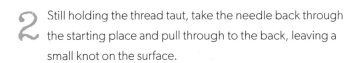
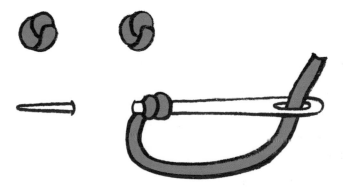

3 Take the needle back up through the fabric at the position of the next knot and repeat the process. French knots can be spaced apart or worked close together in a cluster, or in lines.

APRON WITH POCKETS

PRACTISE SINGLE STITCHES – FLY STITCH, SEED STITCH AND DOUBLE SEED STITCH – ON THE POCKETS OF THIS PRACTICAL APRON, SURE TO DELIGHT ANY DOMESTIC GODDESS. IF YOU'RE NOT CONFIDENT ABOUT SEWING, ATTACH YOUR POCKETS TO A PLAIN SHOP-BOUGHT APRON.

YOU WILL NEED

- Tape measure
- Tailor's chalk
- Thin paper for tracing or photocopying (for method, see page 21)
- Pencil
- All-purpose scissors
- Plain cotton fabric, approximately 14 x 28in (35 x 70cm)
- Erasable marker pen
- Embroidery hoop
- Crewel needle
- Six-stranded embroidery thread, 4 skeins in white
- Iron and pressing cloth
- Fabric scissors
- 1yd (90cm) of spot-print cotton fabric, 45in (112cm) wide
- Sharp needle, or sewing machine
- Sewing thread to match fabric
- Sewing thread in contrast colour, for basting
- Pins

FINISHED SIZE
42½ x 23in (106 x 58.5cm)

TECHNIQUES USED
Running stitch (see page 24)
Fly stitch (see page 74)
Single and double seed stitch (see page 73)

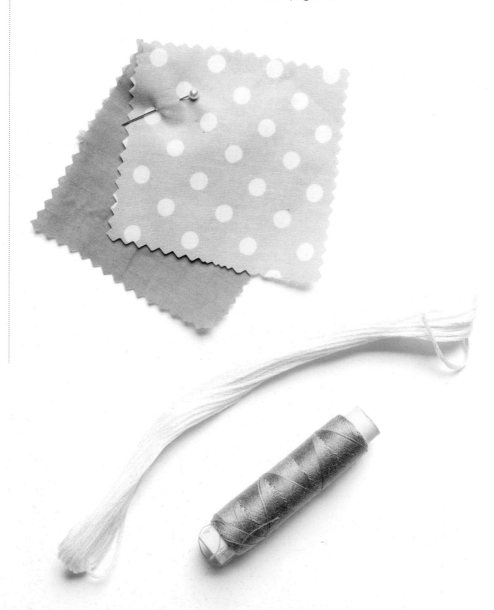

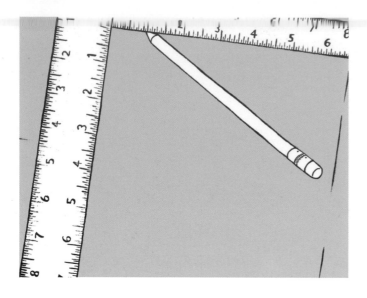

1 Measure and mark out two rectangles, each 10 x 6¼in (25 x 16cm), for the pockets, leaving plenty of space – at least 4in (10cm) – in between.

2 Trace or photocopy the utensils motifs from page 102 on to paper and cut them out to use as templates. Place two on each of the pockets and draw around the outlines with an erasable marker pen.

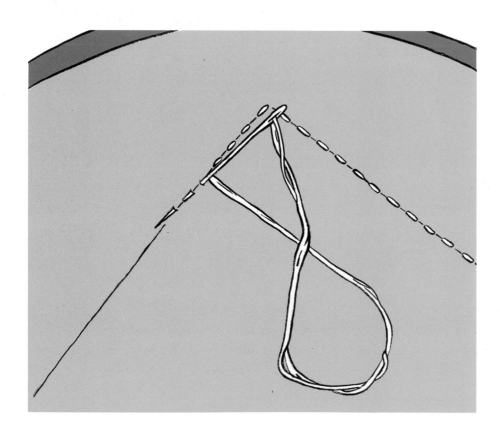

3 Place the fabric in an embroidery hoop, thread a crewel needle with three strands of embroidery thread, and stitch a running stitch around the outline of the pocket.

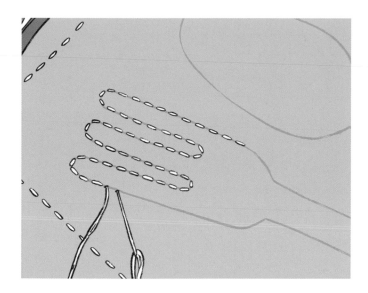

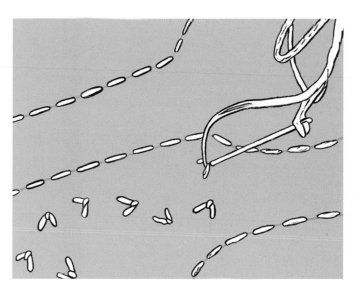

4 Outline each of the utensils in running stitch, with short spaces between the stitches.

5 Embroider fly stitches on the background, around the utensil shapes, spacing the individual fly stitches evenly.

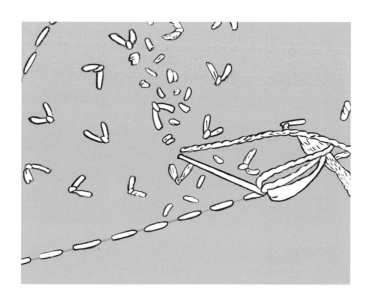

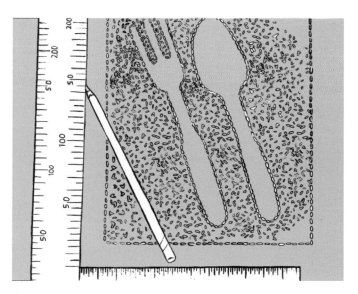

6 Embroider single and double seed stitches between the fly stitches, widening the gaps between the stitches as you work outwards towards the corners and edges of the pocket outline.

7 When the embroidery is complete, remove the fabric from the hoop and press. Measure and mark lines ¾in (2cm) from each side edge and the bottom edge and 2in (5cm) from the top edge, then cut out along these lines.

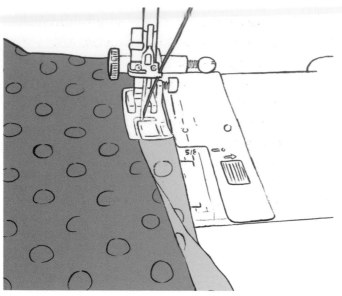

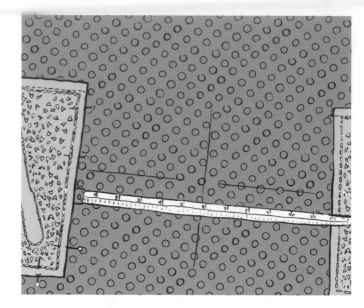

1   Cut the fabric to size: trim the selvedges from the spot-print fabric and cut a piece measuring 24in (60cm) across the whole width of the fabric, for the main part of the apron. Cut two strips 6in (15cm) wide across the whole width, for the waistband, and put these to one side. Hem the two short edges of the main piece, then the lower edge, each with a ½in (1.3cm) double hem. To do this, fold under ½in (1.3cm) and press, then fold under another ½in (1.3cm) and press again. Stitch in place using running stitch or a straight machine stitch.

2   On the pockets, fold ⅜in (1cm) to the wrong side on each side edge and bottom edge and press. On the top edge, fold ½in (1.3cm) to wrong side and press, then a further ¾in (2cm) and press again, to form a double hem. Stitch the hem in place. Fold the apron in half down the centre, then open out. Position each pocket 6in (15cm) either side of centre fold and ½in (1.3cm) up from the lower edge of the apron.

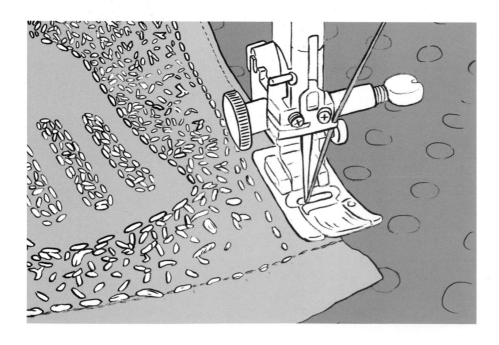

3   Pin and baste the pockets in position, then topstitch (see box, page 83) by hand or machine to hold them securely in place.

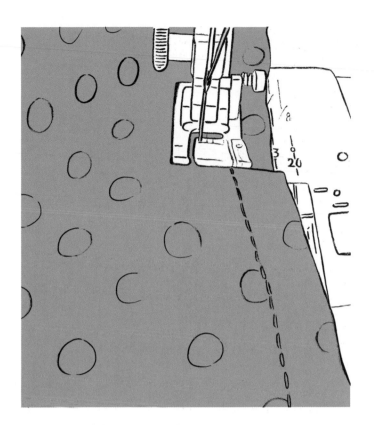

4 Gather the top edge of the apron. To do this by hand, thread a needle with two lengths of sewing thread and sew a running stitch approximately ½–¾in (1.3–2cm) from the top edge. If you are using a sewing machine, sew a line of machine stitching about ½in (1.3cm) from the top edge, then a second line about ¼in (6mm) from the first. Whichever method you choose, at the beginning of the line of stitching, secure the thread ends to the fabric. When you reach the other end, do not fasten off the threads but leave thread ends about 6in (15cm) long.

CUTTING A STRAIGHT LINE

Prints don't always follow the grain of the fabric and are not always a reliable guide when cutting a straight line. For more accurate cutting, use a T-square or similar device to measure and mark right angles.

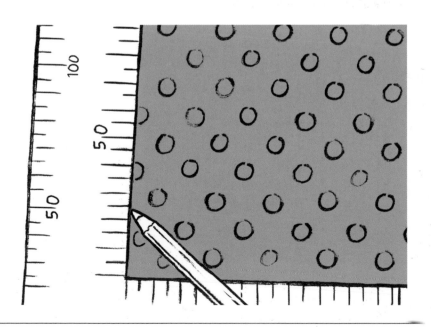

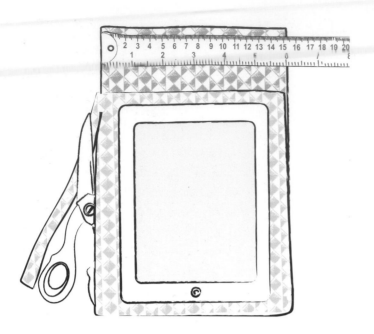

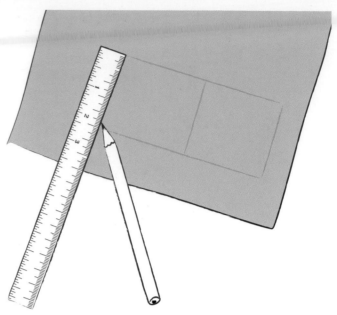

1 Cut the main fabric, lining and wadding to 25¼ x 8⅝in (64 x 22cm), or to fit your tablet (see page 80).

2 Using a ruler and pencil, draw one 4in (10cm) square and four 2in (5cm) squares on the backing paper of the bonding web. Cut out, following the lines you have drawn, then place each one on a different scrap of fabric and bond in place using a hot iron.

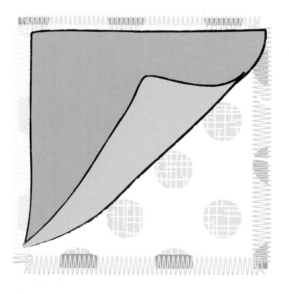

3 Cut out, with a margin of ³⁄₁₆in (5mm) around the edge of the bonding web, then pull several rows of threads out all round, to create a fringed edge.

4 Peel off the backing paper from each piece.

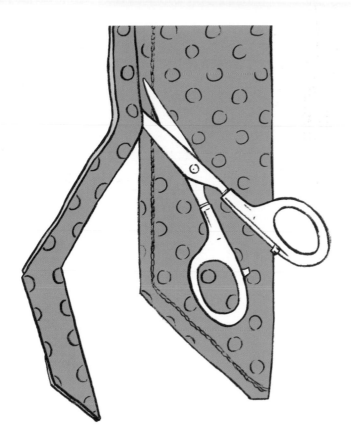 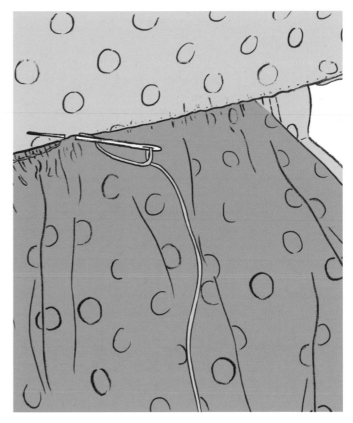

8 Fold the waistband in half and cut across the ends at a 45-degree angle. With a ¾in (2cm) seam allowance, stitch across one short end then along the long edge until the point where the gathering starts, then fasten off. Do the same again, starting at the other short end. Trim seams, then turn the ties right sides out.

9 Turn under ¾in (2cm) along the open edge and press, then slipstitch (see page 25) the folded edge to the seam on the inside of the apron. For a neat finish, topstitch (see below) all round waistband and ties, ⅛in (2–3mm) from edges.

TOPSTITCHING

Topstitching adds a decorative detail and emphasizes seams and edgings for a really crisp finish. It is worked on the right side of the fabric, usually with a longer machine stitch than would be used for a seam. You can use the same weight and colour of thread that you used for the seams, or use a heavier thread in the same colour or a contrasting one. You can also topstitch by hand, using a neat running stitch.

COUCHING

'COUCHING' COMES FROM THE FRENCH *COUCHER*, TO LAY SOMETHING DOWN HORIZONTALLY.
IT IS USED FOR THREADS THAT ARE TOO THICK OR TOO TEXTURED TO PASS THROUGH THE FABRIC
BUT ARE IDEAL FOR LAYING ACROSS THE SURFACE AND HOLDING IN PLACE WITH FINER THREADS.

Couching stitches – the stitches used to hold thicker threads, cords and ribbons in place – can be the same colour as the couched thread or a contrast colour, depending on the effect you wish to achieve. You can work couched threads in straight lines, curves, wavy lines, circles, simple outline motifs or loops. Try out different effects on a piece of spare fabric. The couching stitches can be simple or fancy, straight or diagonal, worked evenly or in clusters. This technique has plenty of scope for creativity.

Tip If you are working a long line of couching, it can help to hold down the thread to be couched by pinning it to the fabric at intervals.

*Couching
(multiple rows)*

Couching (single row)

Blanket stitch

Cross stitch

Herringbone stitch

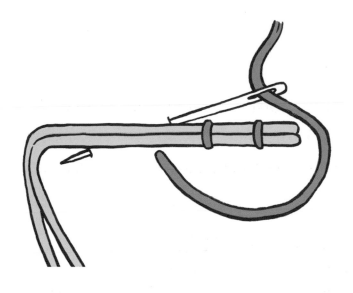

1. Bring the thread to be couched up through the fabric at the beginning of the line. To do this, as long as it is not too thick, thread it into a large-eyed needle. This example shows a double row of couched threads. Thread the needle with the couching thread – usually a finer thread – and make a series of small upright stitches across the thread to be couched, to hold it securely in place.

2. To make a second line of the same thread alongside the first, when you get to the end of the first line, bend the thread to be couched back, take a small stitch across the point where it folds, then work a second line of couching using small straight stitches, as before.

3. To make a loop, or to outline a shape, take the thread in the direction you wish, making couching stitches to hold it in place as you go. In this example, the couching stitches are slanted, rather than straight.

CAFÉ CURTAIN

CAFÉ CURTAINS ARE AN IDEAL WAY OF SCREENING THE LOWER PART OF A WINDOW TO CREATE SOME PRIVACY, AND THEY USE RELATIVELY LITTLE FABRIC. MAKE A FEATURE OF A SMALL CURTAIN LIKE THIS BY DECORATING IT WITH LINES OF COUCHED RIBBONS, CORDS AND BRAID.

YOU WILL NEED

- Tape measure
- Lightweight fabric (see panel on page 88 for quantities)
- Iron
- Sewing thread in contrast colour, for basting
- Sewing thread to match fabric
- Sewing needle (or sewing machine)
- Lengths of braid (such as ric rac), ribbons and cords, a little longer than the width of the curtain
- Pins
- Six-stranded embroidery thread in a selection of colours
- Crewel needle
- All-purpose scissors
- Fabric scissors
- Curtain wire, rod or pole

MATERIAL TO USE

Café curtains can be made of any sheer fabric such as voile or muslin.

TECHNIQUES USED

Running stitch (see page 24)
Backstitch (see page 30)
Blanket stitch (see page 47)
Straight stitch (see page 73)
Couching (see page 85)

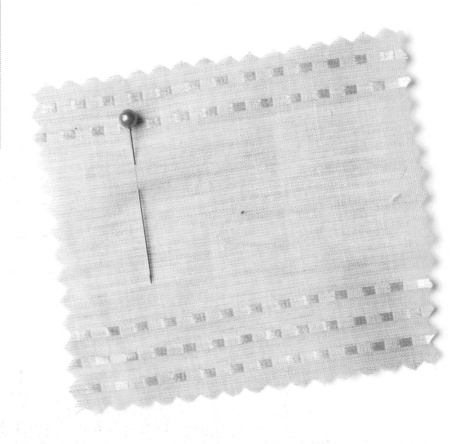

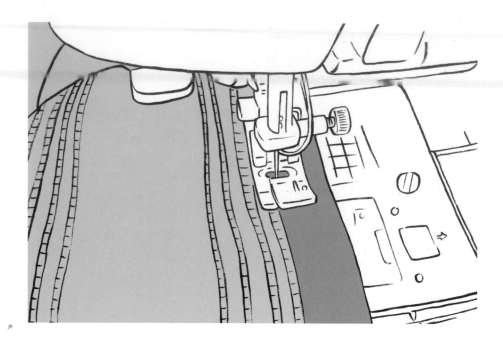

1 On the lower edge of the fabric, fold 1in (2.5cm) to the right side and press. By hand, baste close to the raw edge to hold the hem in place. On a machine, use a straight machine stitch. Press.

2 Pin a length of braid along the stitch line, to cover the raw edge of the hem. Pin another length of braid or ribbon to the curtain, parallel to the first and about 1in (2.5cm) above. Leave a little excess overlapping the side edges of the curtain, which you will trim away later.

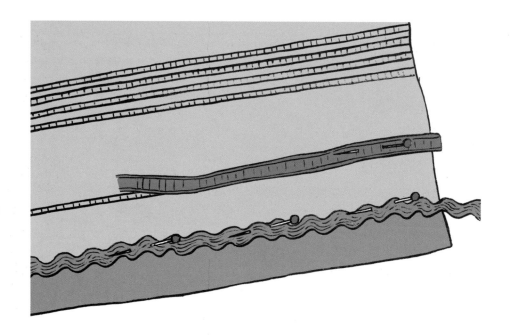

FABRIC QUANTITIES

The amount of fabric you will require depends on the size of your window. Measure the width inside the window recess, to calculate the amount of fabric needed. Multiply this width by 1.5 (or 1.75, or 2, for a fuller effect), then add 2in (5cm) for the side turnings. Measure the length (the 'drop') that you want your curtain to be, then add 2in (5cm) for the hem and casing. The instructions here allow for a narrow casing at the top of the curtain, for inserting a curtain wire. If you are using a rod or pole, allow extra fabric (twice the width of the rod or pole) and make a wider casing.

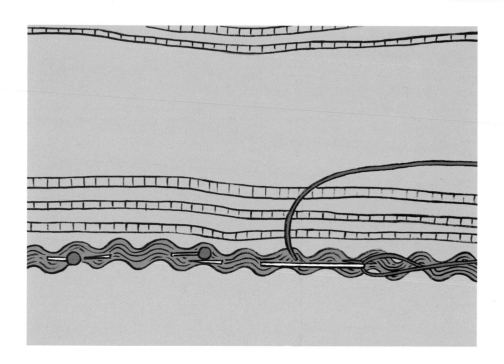

3 Continue pinning further lengths of braid in parallel lines, working upwards, and varying the spacing between each piece. When you are happy with the arrangement, baste each length of ribbon or braid in place, using thread in a contrasting colour.

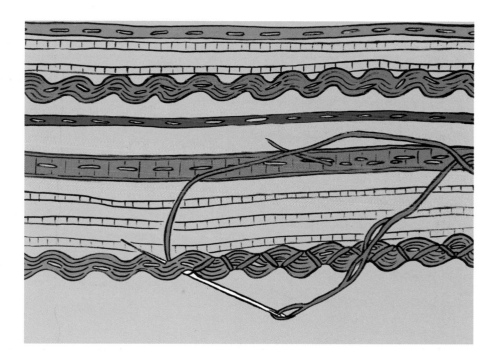

4 Start couching each length of braid using embroidery thread and various embroidery stitches. For ric rac, use backstitch, but instead of working the stitches in a straight line, each stitch should straddle the braid, giving a zigzag line of stitches.

Tip For a neat result on the wrong side of the curtain, when you come to the end of a length of thread, take the needle to the wrong side and run it between the fabric and the braid for about 1in (2.5cm). Snip off the thread close to the fabric.

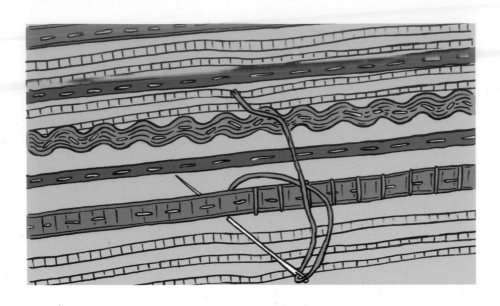

5 For lengths of ribbon with straight edges, start by working straight stitches, evenly spaced, across the width of the ribbon. If you use checked ribbon, this will help you to space the stitches.

6 Re-thread the needle with another coloured thread and, working from right to left, make diagonal stitches, bringing the needle up at the top of one of the upright stitches and down at the bottom of the next stitch to the left. When you reach the other end, make a second row of diagonal stitches, working from left to right, and crossing the previous stitches.

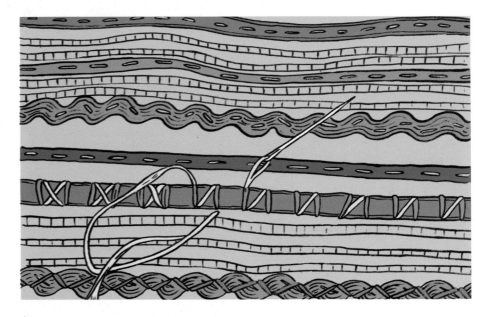

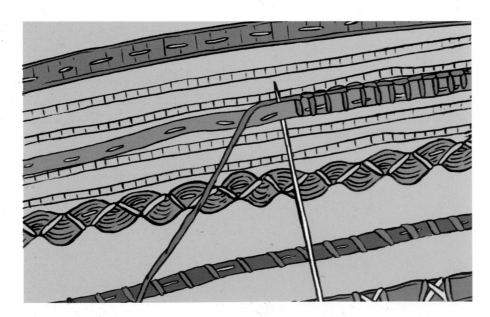

7 Use small, evenly spaced perpendicular stitches to hold down lengths of cord. Couch narrow lengths of ribbon or straight braid using blanket stitch.

CUTWORK

IN CUTWORK, DESIGNS ARE OUTLINED IN BUTTONHOLE STITCH AND AREAS OF FABRIC
ARE THEN CUT AWAY. ALTHOUGH CUTWORK IS TRADITIONALLY WORKED IN WHITE THREAD
ON WHITE FABRIC, WHY NOT BREAK WITH TRADITION AND INTRODUCE SOME COLOUR?

For the best results, use good-quality
linen with a fine weave, or a firm
cotton fabric. The thread can be pearl
cotton or stranded cotton. When
working buttonhole stitch, the stitches
need to be very close together. Before
you start, stretch the fabric in an
embroidery hoop.

BUTTONHOLE STITCH FOR CUTWORK

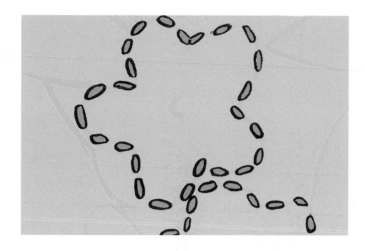

1 Draw the lines of the design using an erasable marker. Thread the needle with a single strand of pearl thread, or two or three strands of stranded thread. Stitch along the design lines in a close running stitch.

2 Bring the needle out on the design line and work as described for blanket stitch (see page 47), but with the stitches touching each other and no fabric showing between the stitches. Each stitch should be perpendicular to the line. The top edge of the stitches – the edge with the rope-like appearance – should surround any areas that are to be cut out.

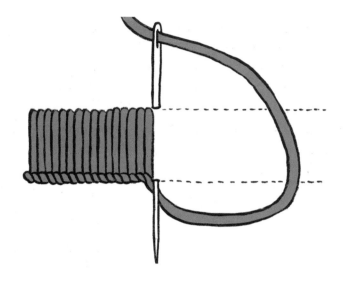

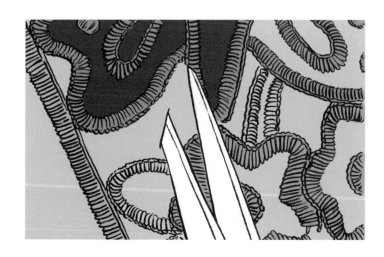

3 When working around a curve, each stitch should still be at right angles to the line. This means that the stitches will splay out slightly, but you should still try to work them as close together as possible.

4 When all the embroidery is complete, press the work carefully on the wrong side, then carefully cut out the 'background' areas of the design using sharp, pointed scissors. Start by piercing the fabric in the centre of the shape, snip towards one corner, then cut the fabric as close to the stitching as possible. Take great care not to snip the stitches.

NEEDLE CASE

THIS NEEDLE CASE DESIGN MAKES A GOOD FIRST CUTWORK PROJECT, AND WHEN YOU
HAVE FINISHED YOU WILL HAVE A PRETTY AND PRACTICAL PLACE TO STORE YOUR NEEDLES,
OR A LOVELY GIFT FOR A SPECIAL FRIEND WHO SHARES YOUR LOVE OF NEEDLEWORK.

YOU WILL NEED

- Closely woven cotton or linen fabric,
  at least 12 x 10in (30 x 25cm)
- Paper for tracing or photocopying
- Erasable marker pen
- Embroidery hoop
- Crewel needle
- Six-stranded embroidery thread,
  1 skein each in pale pink, ochre,
  lavender and eau de nil
- Iron
- Small scissors with sharp points
- Set square
- Cotton fabric in a contrasting colour,
  8 x 4¾in (20 x 12cm)
- Sewing thread to match fabric
- Hand-sewing needle
- Cotton or linen fabric in white, for
  lining, approx 10½ x 7in (26 x 18cm)
- Pinking shears
- Wool or viscose felt, 7 x 4½in
  (18 x 11cm)

FINISHED SIZE

8 x 5in (20 x 12.5cm)

TECHNIQUES USED

Running stitch (see page 24)
Slipstitch (see page 25)
Buttonhole stitch for cutwork
(see page 93)
Satin stitch (see page 63)

Tip To transfer the motif
on to the fabric you can use
a light box, but you will need
to trace or photocopy the design
on to plain paper first.

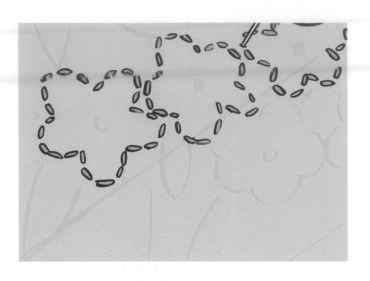

1 Fold the white fabric in half. Trace or photocopy the design from page 99 and place on a light box or tape to a window. Place the fabric on top and, using an erasable marker pen, trace the design on to the fabric, to the right of the fold. Place the fabric in an embroidery hoop so that the whole design fits into the hoop. Thread a crewel needle with a single strand of pale pink thread and outline each of the flower shapes in running stitch, just inside the design line.

2 Using a single strand of thread, work buttonhole stitch all around each flower shape. Change to ochre thread and work running stitch all around the rectangular frame, then work buttonhole stitch on top. Change to lavender thread and work running stitch all round the outline of the butterfly, its body and the petal shapes on the wings. Work buttonhole stitch all around these shapes and satin stitch to fill the small dots on the wings.

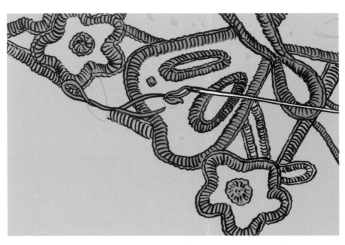

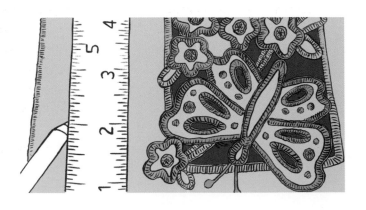

3 Change to eau de nil thread and work running stitch, then buttonhole stitch, to outline the leaf shapes. Remove the work from the hoop and press lightly on the reverse. Carefully cut out the background areas of the design, taking care not to snip the stitches.

4 Measure and trim the fabric to 10½ x 7in (26 x 18cm), making sure the original fold is in the centre and the cutwork embroidery is centred on the right-hand half of the fabric. Fold in half and press along the fold.

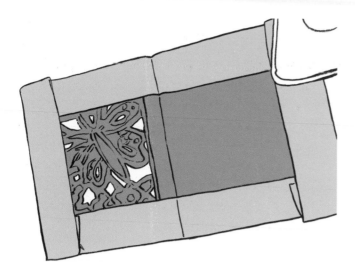

5 Fold in 1in (2.5cm) to the wrong side all the way round to make a hem. Press the folded edge.

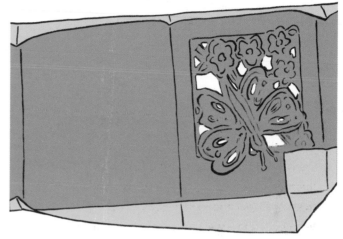

6 Open out the hem, then fold down each corner in turn, lining up the crease marks. Press the corners.

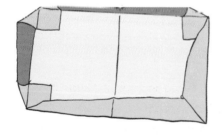

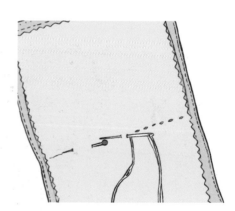

7 Place the contrast fabric centrally on the wrong side of the embroidered fabric, to form a lining, and fold each of the corners down, on top of the lining, then fold over each edge, creating a neat mitre at each corner. Slipstitch the folded edges together on each corner.

8 Sew a running stitch around the edges, through all layers, using sewing thread to match the fabric. Turn under ½in (1.3cm) all around the white lining fabric. Place it centrally on the inside of the needle case, covering the contrast lining, and slipstitch the edges to the main fabric all the way round.

9 Trim the edges of the felt with pinking shears. Place the felt centrally on the inside of the needle case and stitch in place down the centre, through all the layers, with a neat running stitch.

TEMPLATES AND PATTERNS

THE TEMPLATES AND MOTIFS ON THESE PAGES WILL NEED TO BE PHOTOCOPIED ON TO PLAIN PAPER.

WHERE THEY NEED TO BE ENLARGED, THE PERCENTAGE IS GIVEN.

SHIRT TATTOO MOTIF
Copy at 100%

NEEDLE CASE MOTIF
Copy at 100%

*Cut away
shaded areas*

TEA COSY TEMPLATE

Copy at 200%

TEA COSY MOTIF

Copy at 200%

KANTHA CUSHION MOTIF
Copy at 150%

APRON WITH POCKETS MOTIF

Copy at 100%

BIRD PICTURE
Copy at 200%

Stockists and websites

The Cotton Patch

Fabrics and haberdashery

www.cottonpatch.co.uk

DMC

Embroidery threads and fabrics

www.dmccreative.co.uk

Madeira

Embroidery threads and accessories

www.madeira.co.uk

Mez Crafts

Embroidery threads and fabrics

www.mezcrafts.co.uk

The Purl Bee

Online embroidery tutorials

www.purlsoho.com

Sarah's Hand Embroidery

Online embroidery tutorials

www.embroidery.rocksea.org

Sew and So

Haberdashery and embroidery supplies

www.sewandso.co.uk

Sewing Online

Haberdashery and embroidery supplies

www.sewing-online.com

About the author

Artist, writer and designer Susie Johns grew up in a household where drawing and making things were very much encouraged – both of her parents and all four of her grandparents were creative people.

Having studied Fine Art at the Slade School, London, Susie began her publishing career as a magazine and partworks editor before becoming a freelance writer and designer. She is the author of more than 30 craft books – including *How to Sew, How to Machine Sew* and *Knitted Woodland Creatures* – on a range of subjects including knitting, crochet, papier mâché and embroidery. Susie has also contributed to a number of magazines, such as *Let's Knit, Crafts Beautiful, Embroidery* and *Needlecraft*. She particularly enjoys art and craft activities that involve recycling and reinventing.

Susie is a qualified teacher and runs workshops in drawing and painting, knitting and crochet, embroidery and 3D design near her home in Greenwich, London.

Acknowledgements

Many thanks to the following for their help in creating this book: Jonathan Bailey, for asking me to do it in the first place; Andrew Perris for the attractive photography and styling; Martin Woodward and Joshua Brent for the lovely illustrations; Chloë Alexander, for designing the finished book so that it looks so inviting; Cath Senker for her attention to detail in editing the text; and Sara Harper for her support and organizational skills.

Index

To order a book, or to request
a catalogue, contact:

GMC Publications Ltd
Castle Place, 166 High Street,
Lewes, East Sussex,
BN7 1XU
United Kingdom
Tel: +44 (0)1273 488005
www.gmcbooks.com